A Soldier's Home

For permissions, bulk ordering, or speaking engagements
contact the author at: www.scrafoundation.org
Published in collaboration with
Season Press and Fortitude Graphic Design and Printing
Design and layout by Sean Hollins-Fortitude Graphic Design
Author photo by Deborah McCaw

Library of Congress Control Number: 2016944652

Cooper, Matthew R.
A Soldier's Home: United States Servicemembers vs. Wall Street
p.cm
1. Law-Military 2. Foreclosure-Banks
3. Soldiers-History

ISBN-10: 0-9977136-0-7
ISBN-13: 978-0-9977136-0-2

Printed in the United States of America

FIRST EDITION
10 9 8 7 6 5 4 3 2 1

This book is dedicated to my family, and all of the men and women who have, and will serve our country.

M.C.

Table of Contents

FOREWORD

In the Spring of 2008, I received a telephone call one day from Matt Cooper, a lawyer in Paw Paw, Michigan, concerning a case he was handling involving a Michigan National Guard soldier named James Hurley. Since a significant amount of my law practice deals with the Servicemembers Civil Relief Act (the successor statute to the Soldiers' and Sailors' Civil Relief Act), such calls were not particularly unusual, but this one was. Matt was struggling to get a federal court in Grand Rapids to understand the nature of his cause of action on behalf of Sergeant Hurley. When I was contacted, the case had been dismissed.

Because Matt was so adamant that his client's home had been illegally foreclosed I listened carefully. I realized almost immediately that a violation of the SCRA had, in fact, taken place and that dismissal of the suit had been erroneous. I agreed to help Matt draft a motion for reconsideration of the dismissal ruling, but my primary role at that point was to be an expert witness on interpretation of the SCRA. When that first motion to reconsider was denied by the court, we went into the "if at first you don't succeed, try and try again" mode and filed a second motion to reconsider (to point out, as carefully as possible, that the case the court had cited to deny the motion for reconsideration had subsequently been vacated and set aside and the Michigan court's ruling was not based on sound precedent). Telling a federal judge that his law clerk missed something is not something I had significant experience doing and I was not anxious to further antagonize the court.

At long last, the court set aside its prior erroneous rulings and granted summary judgment in favor of Sergeant Hurley. By that time, my role in the case had morphed from potential expert witness to full-blown co-counsel for Sergeant Hurley. Matt and his dedicated co-counsel, Frank Melchiore, kept pushing the case until we finally became what is believed to be the first SCRA case to ever actually go to jury trial in a federal courtroom. The case settled after the fifth day of a jury trial and we were all pleased to have won a significant victory for our clients.

i

Hurley v. Deutsche Bank Trust Company Americas became the basis for an amendment to the SCRA that clearly provides that there is a private cause of action to sue for damages and other relief when a servicemember's rights under the Act have been violated. I can honestly say that without the dedication and doggedness of Matt Cooper, the amendment to the SCRA that has made justice possible for so many other servicemembers would have been delayed in coming, if it came at all.

Without lawyers like Matt Cooper being willing to take on the big banks, servicemembers will never get the justice they deserve. It was my privilege to work with him on the *Hurley* case and I think you will enjoy reading of his saga.

John S. Odom, Jr., Colonel, USAF (ret.)

Shreveport, Louisiana

PREFACE

Sergeant James Hurley was a twenty-five-year Michigan National Guard soldier when he was sent to Iraq in 2004. Despite the fact that he had family obligations, the lovable and easy-going man in his 40s, obeyed his orders for deployment. During President George W. Bush's surge, he was stationed in Iraq, on a base that became known as the "Bloody Triangle."

For more than ten years, Hurley enjoyed his dream home. To him, it was a paradise set deep in majestic woods on a high ridge along the Paw Paw River in Michigan. However, while he was away at war, a foreign bank violated U.S. law and illegally took his home. The bank forced Hurley's mother, wife, and two small children from their home. After he served for one year, he made it out alive. But 844 American service members would not be so lucky; they lost their lives in Iraq in 2005. Hurley returned from the war, but when he got home, another family was living in his home. He now would have to fight a war on the home front.

One of our world's largest banks, and its lawyers, conspired to illegally take Hurley's dream home. It would take years of court action, and a trial that mirrored a Grisham novel, to uncover a scheme that violated soldiers' rights and federal law. *A Soldier's Home,* follows Hurley from his tranquil life at home, through his tour in Iraq. The story culminates with the legal odyssey of the illegal acts of the lenders and lawyers who seized his home and removed his family. The "say or do anything" litigation tactics to cover up mortgage foreclosure policies (that violated the rights of thousands of U.S. soldiers), are set forth in this landmark legal drama.

Sergeant Hurley would become the subject of a Federal Court lawsuit that would—after years of legal battle—result in Congressional Amendments that benefit *all* servicemembers in the United States Military. Hurley took on one of the world's largest banks in a David vs. Goliath campaign that lasted seven years and resulted in the first jury trial of its kind.

As a result, the Department of Justice obtained the largest Service-members Civil Relief Act (SCRA) settlement in its history following the groundwork set by the Hurley case. General Petraeus, his wife Holly, and Hurley addressed the problem of banks foreclosing on the homes of active duty soldiers. It was a topic with Katie Couric on the *CBS Evening News*, *National Public Radio* with Adam Hochberg, and even with Senator Hillary Clinton who held a press conference about the matter. Diane Sawyer of *ABC News, Fox and Friends,* and many major newspapers in the world, discussed Hurley and the foreclosure crisis as it related to soldiers. The *Malaysian Sun* poked fun at the United States, which allowed Hurley to fall prey to the interests of a foreign bank.

Protections that started with our Nation's independence have been strengthened with congressional action known as the Hurley Amendments. When the United States sends its men and women away to fight in a war, their homes should be protected. President Lincoln and the Servicemembers Civil Relief Act (SCRA) agree that U.S. soldiers willingly sign up with the understanding that they may make the ultimate sacrifice for their country. At the same time, they do not sacrifice and fight for a country that allows others to violate their civil rights or take advantage of them while they perform their military duties.

Hurley's Federal District Court action is the first time a jury was seated to hear such a case. The U.S. banks typically support troops and followed the SCRA. But a foreign bank tested our country's resolve. The U.S. Department of Justice monitored the Hurley case for years and brought actions on behalf of hundreds of soldiers. Attorney Matthew R. Cooper, of Paw Paw, Michigan, represented Hurley and his family. Their Federal District Court action marked the first time a jury would be seated to hear such a case.

Hurley and his family brought action against Deutsche Bank, (one of the world's largest banks) Saxon Mortgage Company (one of our country's largest mortgage serving companies), and a Detroit foreclosure law office. Over the five years of meandering litigation through the federal court system, Cooper assembled one of the greatest litigation teams to litigate a SCRA case. Colonel John S. Odom, Jr. and Colonel Gregory Huckabee (drafters of the SCRA), were priceless allies. Litigators, Frank B. Melchiore and Daniel G. Romano, also were instrumental in Hurley's success.

The story of James Hurley is one of "what ifs." *What if* a financial institution and its agents do not follow the law? *What if* a soldier goes off to war, surrounded by death and destruction, and his wife, children, and mother are removed from their home?

THE HURLEY CASE AND THE HISTORY OF LINCOLN'S 21ST CENTURY SOLDIERS

More than 150 years ago, President Abraham Lincoln implemented protections for United States Soldiers from predatory lenders while they were at war protecting our Country. General George Washington said, "When we assumed the soldier we did not lay aside the Citizen."

At the conception of our Nation our soldiers' sacrifices were understood and recognized. During the Civil War, President Abraham Lincoln protected his soldiers from predatory lenders. He expanded upon General Washington's protections and formulated national legislation. Jefferson Davis did the same for the Confederacy. For more than 150 years, the United States of America has continued to provide our soldiers with similar protections. This support for soldiers began with President Washington, and continued through the support of President Lincoln, the Soldiers and Sailors Civil Relief Act of 1918, and today's Servicemembers Civil Relief Act.

When our country went off to war in World War I, these protections were codified by Federal Act in the Soldiers and Sailors Civil Relief Act. (SSCRA). These protections are now known as the Servicemembers' Civil Relief Act (SCRA). The Servicemembers Civil Relief Act states as its purpose "to provide for, strengthen, and expedite the national defense through protection by this act to Servicemembers of the United States..."

Following the Cold War (and in particular the wars in Afghanistan and Iraq), the United States Military has drawn heavily from our soldiers in the National Guard, where Hurley served for twenty-five years. Like Hurley, soldiers from all walks of life, and from all age brackets, are taken from their daily lives as ordinary citizens and thrown into the heat of battles and the heart of war zones. These folks may one day appear as an ordinary citizen—a local banker working on personal loans during the day and coaching youth baseball in the evenings—and the next week, are in Iraq on a search for hidden explosives.

That may seem overly dramatic, but it is a mere example that plays itself out time and time again, for those of various backgrounds and professions, and at the same time, are of the highest skill set individuals our military has ever seen. Regular drills and extended training details allow this military to consist of the Citizen Soldier. These Citizen Soldiers are not a new concept.

President Abraham Lincoln drew from a similar lot of common citizens for the Civil War, which may have (at that time) been the most dramatic time period where the citizens who served as soldiers were most highly prevalent and significantly needed and utilized. On both sides of the war, ordinary citizens were called to service. Many Civil War soldiers were called away for years. There were no phones, or Skype for these soldiers. When they were away from home, they were gone. Letters were sporadic and cumbersome. Communication between a soldier and those back home could not effectively address real-time issues.

The Civil War lasted longer than anyone planned. Soldiers were away much longer than they thought or planned. Just as today, people in the nineteenth century had bills to pay and relied upon their regular income to pay their debts. A Citizen Soldier's life, then as now, was thrown into an upheaval of trying to make ends meet when there is a break in sporadic pay. Just as today, when bills were not paid 150 years ago, creditors would pursue debtors for their money. Debt collectors and lawyers would hound people for payment.

Presidents Lincoln and Jefferson Davis recognized this dire situation for soldiers and their families. War is hell with mutilation, injury, and death. For the survivors, the reality of life continues. Debts must be paid and families taken care of. Both Lincoln and Davis enacted legislation to protect their soldiers from bill collectors and lawsuits.

In 1918, the United States enacted the Soldiers' and Sailors' Civil Relief Act (SSCRA). Throughout World War I, II, Korea, Vietnam, and the Gulf War, active duty servicemembers and their families have been protected by the SSCRA. The Act simply gives the servicemember time. Debts and responsibilities still exist, but while they are off serving their country God knows where, they cannot be sued or collected against. No soldier should go off to war and return to find that the home they left, no longer belongs to them.

The men and women serving in the United States Military should have the opportunity to focus all of their energy and efforts on their war. If there is cause for foreclosing on a soldier's home, the process cannot take place until they are able to be back home and be allowed to defend themselves. The Soldiers' and Sailors' Civil Relief Act for much of our history, and now the Servicemembers' Civil Relief Act, allows soldiers this opportunity.

Lincoln's Civil War Soldiers are much like the soldiers in our military today—a member of the community. Married and with children, these soldiers are older and more established than a World War I or World War II draftee. They are more likely to have debts or mortgages, much like the U.S. soldiers in Iraq and Afghanistan. This uniquely older, debt-ridden, mortgage-bound soldier of today is exactly what should be expected when drawing upon our citizenry for soldiers.

In 2003, the Soldiers' and Sailors' Civil Relief Act was updated, amended and renamed the Servicemembers' Civil Relief Act or SCRA. The SCRA contained the same protections against creditors that Congress set forth in 1918, and what Lincoln and Davis did during the Civil War. A soldier, while serving for the United States of America, should have the protections that allow them to concentrate and focus on their war effort. When they come home, they can deal with their private, civilian affairs.

Lincoln's 21st Century Soldiers are not the teenagers or the young men and women our country is so in debt to, who fought during WWI, WWII, Korea, and Vietnam. Similar to the Revolutionary and Civil War Veteran, today's soldiers are mature adults with families, careers, and mortgages. They have come to be referred to in the twenty-first century as "Citizen Soldiers.

Attorney Matthew R. Cooper

Acknowledgement

The Hurley case is so important to our servicemembers and their families. Sean and Sonya Hollins of Season Press, LLC have sure done justice in helping me tell of this landmark SCRA case. I would like to thank them for thier expertise in graphic design and editorial consultation.

A Soldier's Home

The
Landmark
Hurley
Case

Matthew R. Cooper

Season Press

CHAPTER
THE BLOODY TRIANGLE

Sergeant James Hurley was a twenty-five-year veteran of the Michigan National Guard. He was a true Citizen Soldier. Despite his years of service, he had never been activated to a war zone, until 2004. That year, he was called on by President George W. Bush, and found himself in the hottest zone of the Iraq War. It was President Bush's surge that would decide the fate of the war.

Hurley was one of the "lucky ones." He was not ordered to fly into Iraq, but chosen to drive across the war-torn country from Kuwait in a large tanker truck filled with explosive fuel. He felt as though he had just jumped head first into a blast furnace. The heat was excruciatingly painful and nothing like he had ever felt before. For a veteran welder use to working in the hottest conditions, he realized that this was going to be a whole new experience.

He ran faster than he had ever run before as he crossed packed sand, the dust clouds everywhere. The 45-year-old soldier had just arrived at his base in Iraq. He had only been there for thirty seconds. Before getting to the wall that he hoped to use for cover, the explosion took the ground from beneath him. He found himself face down in a pile of flaming debris, the tanker truck he had just driven, was struck by a Rocket Propelled Grenade (RPG). The insurgents had been tracking him for days—ever since he had crossed the border.

The Iraqi warriors waited for Hurley to get to the base so that the explosion would take out more targets at once. The edginess and fear

Sgt. Hurley had felt over the last three days was justified. As he lie on the vibrating ground, he recalled the reports of returning veterans and the word around the guard unit in Greenville, that his unit would have a straight-forward departure from the United States to their base in Iraq.

Modern-day travel had made the whole thing seem surreal. After he left the United States and boarded a few connecting flights, he had become a foreigner on foreign land…in a war zone. Hurley recalled his superior officer sarcastically reporting to him that he was selected as, "one of the lucky ones," for his travel accommodations. The Greenville Unit was shipped out shortly after the Bush surge in Iraq.

In 2004, the war was going badly. The level of insurgency was great and troop levels were low and hit hard. That was coupled with no weapons of mass destruction, no tubes…nothing that the Bush Administration hoped to prove their cause for invasion. The intelligence community's integrity was shaken down to a level where recovery was questionable.

There was an inability to control all of the intelligence communities and get them to work together. The United States had to prevail. The Bush surge in late 2004 through 2005 meant win or lose. Hurley was among the few from each unit selected to be part of a convoy that would drive from Kuwait to their destination in Iraq—no connecting flights. With the surge, there was a need for additional equipment and supplies, and these new soldiers would be charged with the delivery.

Hurley and the others in the convoy were to meet up with their units in about three days; where they were going really didn't matter. One desolate part of the desert looked like any other, but getting there was going to be a scary and unpleasant experience. Three days and nights were spent in a convoy headed in and out of enemy hostile territory. Danger seemed always present.

The convoy departed from Kuwait at nightfall, as instructed. From Kuwait, they would travel in complete darkness for three nights, stopping during the day for sleep. But, not many would sleep in the desert during the day in a convoy, which drove through strange and dangerous territory. From Kuwait, they headed to what came to be known as the "Bloody Triangle" at a base between Baghdad and Fallujah. It was an area named Al-Taqaddum, or as the soldiers came to refer to it as, TQ.

Hurley drove in a semi-truck hauling a tanker full of fuel. Not only did he have a constant concern of attack, he was in the nose of a giant bomb. He felt he never knew where he was as he drove through the never-ending desert. As darkness came to an end, the soldiers in the convoy stopped where they were—no exits, no landmarks, just on the road—in hopes to secure themselves.

Chow was simply what food items each soldier had on them at the time, and sleep was where they could get out of the sun, and find comfort in their vehicle. But, to sleep next to a tanker full of fuel, in a war zone, in open daylight, not knowing exactly where they were was hardly relaxing. The most comfortable spot for Hurley was between the semi-tractor and the hitch for the tanker. There he could stretch out or curl up, like his old dog in the back of a pick-up truck.

He especially liked to look up at the desert sky. During the night, the deserted conditions made him feel they were driving on the moon through outer space with all of the stars around them. While it was very disconcerting, Hurley felt if they were to take a hit, it would be over before he even knew what happened. He tried not to think about what he was driving and where.

After the second day, he was easily distracted by the thoughts of some hot chow. The lucky ones chosen for this convoy duty were frequently reminded of the hot chow that awaited them at their new base. There would be much gratitude bestowed upon them for making the drive. Hurley and his driving partner frequently escaped the pressure with talk of home. He reminisced of fishing and hunting, his old dog Buck, and the duck hunting he would do on the Paw Paw River. Whoever would listen about Brandie, and the girls, and their connections to the Michigan wilderness, would become the audience to some fantastic tale about his home.

The Hurley property provided much activity for everyone who was invited. They took great pride in living off the land. Their property produced the meat for most of their meals through turkey and deer hunting. This part of the Paw Paw River supplied an abundant supply of salmon, which came from Lake Michigan. Every spare moment from work or his duties with the National Guard were spent hunting, fishing, or building something on his property. He constructed a gazebo that overlooked the river, a workshop for all of his projects, a garage for storage, and a barn for more storage.

Shortly after departing Kuwait, the convoy came upon a scene of much death and carnage from roadside bombs. It was a very real and immediate touch of reality for the journey across no man's land, and being in a tanker only seemed to accentuate the danger and volatility of the situation. After night three, everyone's nerves had been so buffed and numb that all the men could do was think of hot chow and settling into their new quarters. They had gone several days without a meal and were hungry and tired. The edginess from the start and through the last couple of nights, were gone. This was an assignment that required one to mentally remove oneself from the situation and circumstances. There was constant fighting and killing.

But, in the last rest period, Hurley found himself in a deep sleep that caused him to reflect on one of his last days back home. It was a beautiful summer day in Southwest Michigan, as pleasant as any other place in the world. The warmth of the sun was cooled by a frequent breeze. He had built a private sanctuary deep in the woods, surrounded by a flowing river and a slow moving stream. Just as most other pleasant days, there was the sound of the wind rustling through the trees, trickling river water, and country music that played on the radio.

The tranquility of the moment was broken by painful yelps of another memory. He had just cracked his knuckles on the under carriage of his 62' Chevy pick-up truck, in a restoration project that had become a labor of love. He had a '65 Chevy long wheel-base that he was using for parts in the conversion of his '62 Chevy Step Side. It was his pride and joy. He looked forward to the day he could complete it to display in the

Hartford Strawberry Fest Parade. He imagined his wife Brandie up front with him in the cab, and their two girls Autumn and Jacqueline in the back, waiving U.S. flags.

The Chevy would be stored in a custom built workshop that he made from the ground up, just for the truck. The garage was for his everyday transportation vehicle with an attached shed just for his tools. Before heading off to Iraq he prepared it for storage. Those dreams would all have to wait.

The Hurley property sat on ten acres that, due to its isolation, seemed more like a thousand. The entire parcel was set among rolling hills and hardwoods on the peninsula surrounded by the Paw Paw River. Their home sat high on a ridge over looking the river and had an enclosed porch on the back deck. No other homes could be seen, and seldom was another person ever sighted, except for the occasional canoe or kayak that coasted down the slow moving river.

Around the back of the property was a stream that created the peninsula-like setting. The home and buildings sat unseen from the roadway. A long-winding driveway ran from the road through a thick woods. He discovered the property when canoeing the river with a friend. James noticed the beauty of a building site immediately. While the home itself started as a pre-fabricated structure, it soon was transformed. There was a spectacular panoramic river view out the back picture window, a deck, gazebo, screened-in porch, floating docks, tire swing and a river rope. The Hurley compound just kept growing as a result of a man that could build and do anything with his own two hands.

He felt that this was his paradise and he was living a dream. The best place he has ever lived. For ten years he built the place up and never missed a mortgage payment. In addition, his mother Valla lived with them, and action was being taken to adopt Brandie's two daughters. They were young, just a baby and a toddler when James married their mother. He was the only father the two girls had ever known. This was the only home they knew, and the best place Brandie had ever lived.

She had come from a broken home; one foster care placement after another. She was close to continuing that cycle for her own daughters when James came into her life. It was the first time she experienced a family. The Hurley home was the best of everything for all of them. As James worked at a cheese factory, Brandie was a stay-at-home mom.

Before deployment, James was anxious to get the Chevy stored away as his mother, his brother Steven, and friends came by for his farewell party. He knew that he needed to slow down and concentrate on his grip on the socket, as he didn't want to crack his knuckles again. After he got everything sealed and ready for storage, he put dryer sheets throughout the engine compartment and throughout the vehicle to keep the mice out. He looked forward to some day being able to complete the project. Later that day, James and his guests enjoyed a home-cooked meal and some cold beer, knowing it would be some time before they would see each other again. They all enjoyed the property, which was the focal point for many family gatherings.

***

Loud crackling radio traffic awoke Hurley from his slumber. He heard over the radio that they needed to move. Soon they would be approaching their base, TQ. Al-Taqaddum is in the middle of the Bloody Triangle, but they had made it with a tanker full of fuel. He was feeling lucky and ready for the hot chow that he had been thinking about for a couple of days. As he got out of the truck and even before unpacking in his new quarters, he headed to the mess hall.

Just as he grabbed his tray and headed for the food, he heard gunfire. Everyone took off running. Just as Hurley reached a speed faster than he was sure he had ever run before, an RPG slammed into what had been his sleeping platform for the past three days. He heard and felt what was the largest explosion and sensation that he has ever felt—let alone imagined.

For three days and nights, they traveled through what felt like and appeared to be another planet. There were desolate, deserted stretches of desert highway and communities unlike he had ever seen before...

sights of a war. Mutilated buildings and machinery, people dressed in garments looked unlike none he had ever seen. All he desired was to get safely where they were going. He just wanted to get back with the rest of his unit and find out his mission. After getting out of his convoy tractor-trailer, he stored his personal effects and tools near where he was directed. He saw what was going to be assigned as his quarters. It was a small building, dormitory style. He was thinking about how he may try to make some connection back home, shower, and settle into his new quarters after he got something to eat. The attack upon his arrival was a clear sign of where he was in Iraq and what the next year would be like. Hurley needed to settle in to what—for the next year—would be his new home.

Back in Michigan, Hurley had lived a comfortable and financially secure life. His security was due to the fact that he always worked and never missed a week's paycheck. While Hurley had spent his last twenty-five years with the Michigan National Guard at the post in Fort Custer (Battle Creek), he had recently accepted an assignment to the Greenville Post. That post was being activated and sent to Iraq, and they needed volunteer transfers from around the state. Hurley felt compelled to help with their efforts in Iraq.

Although he was originally assigned and trained as a welder (something he did for a living), he was being trained and reassigned as a generator mechanic. Having to leave his employment in the Cheese Factory and go to California for training in anticipation of his deployment for Operation Iraqi Freedom caused a serious interruption in the Hurley family cash flow. For ten years, the priority payment was his mortgage payment. He scrapped by for weeks without a paycheck, but it seemed impossible to make the payment. However, they were able to manage by pulling together as a family.

The California training served as a good trial run for everyone. Hurley fell naturally into his training as a generator mechanic. He was being trained as an army mechanic for large generators. This was a natural for him as he had worked on some kind of engine his entire life. As a welder, he was even able to fabricate some tools that he would take with him to Iraq. The mechanics that came back from Iraq, shared with him some of the difficulties with tools the army provided. Ever the optimist and handyman, he was excited for the challenges ahead of him and was going to Iraq prepared and with the tools that he would need to get the job done.

While Hurley was in California, Valla moved in with Brandie and the girls. She worked as a home care aid for the elderly and homebound with the State of Michigan. Her paycheck helped make ends meet, and her stay with Brandie for a couple of months was a good trial run for his tour in Iraq. The Hurley home had plenty of space for everyone, and Valla's income was a great supplement. The freezers were well stocked with venison, turkey, squirrel, rabbit, duck and salmon; all taken right from the Hurley backyard.

Brandie and the girls loved having Valla stay with them. Beyond the obvious financial assistance, the two ladies were cut from the same cloth. They were survivors. Spoiled to them meant having electricity, a sound roof, heat, food, and clothing for the kids. The Hurley home was all of this and much more. They were ready for the departure. They were strong for him; loved their country and felt a sense of pride and honor to keep the home front in order for their soldier. Hurley had worked for years to achieve such a wonderful homestead and the Hurley women would keep it safe for his return.

CHAPTER
TQ

After the explosion, everyone took cover. All James could do was try to join up with his fellow soldiers from his unit. Others from his unit had been in TQ for a few days, and had learned the bunker system, and what the mechanics were expected to do when under attack. The command post and small hospital had to have power. While the initial reaction is to take cover and help in the defense of the propelling attack, the generator power mechanics had to keep the flow of electrical power. Generators and lines ran throughout the command center. A single generator the size of a Greyhound bus could run a field hospital.

Mechanics like Hurley were expected to always make sure the "juice" was flowing. They were expected to actually climb inside these massive generators and crawl around like mice in a maze. Hurley was an expert in working his way through the bowels of these massive machines, and took great pride in his ability to keep the power on. He was like a precision surgeon with his tools, and was an expert at diagnosing and fixing problems.

As an experienced welder, he had added abilities and knowledge to supplement his new trade and training as a mechanic. While he was prepared with the custom tools (that he had purchased with his own money in the states), he was able to actually weld and fabricate specialty tools needed for specific repairs and maintenance tasks he learned were necessary to keep the generators running. He took great pride in his ability to fabricate, and shared his custom tools with his fellow soldiers. Frequently, tools he made were left with the specific machinery, even as he moved on to another job. Others would benefit from the expertise and generosity of Sgt. Hurley.

When he gathered himself after the explosion and subsequent chaos, he was immediately relieved that he had removed his personal effects, and the tools that he had brought with him, from the truck. He was grateful of the advice given to him back home by returning soldiers, who told him what tools he should bring, that were not part of the standard-issue generator mechanics tool chest.

Once things calmed down from the tanker explosion, Hurley learned of his bunk assignment. He was assigned to a small dormitory-style room with three other mechanics. Once he settled in, he learned the Iraqis probably had a bead on his truck as a prize target. They may have waited until he left Kuwait to attack once he got to the command center, because that would give the enemy the highest probability of causing the most destruction. It was a chilling thought that he was driving a massive bomb for the enemy. Had he understood at the time, he may have had less anxiety and worry about driving across the war-torn country, and more focus on knowing that he was under constant surveillance by the enemy.

After three days of traveling across Iraq, and the "Welcome to Iraq" RPG attack, Hurley quickly settled into his new bunk and enjoyed the company of his fellow mechanics. The mechanics quarters were not too far from the bunker system. It was quite an experience to sit along the bunkers, and watch the rockets and their streaming red flames crisscross the desert sky between Baghdad and Fallujah in the evenings. Through it all, his priority was to have regular contact with Brandie and the girls back home.

Family and home is always on a soldier's mind. It is that commitment to family, home, and country, that is a primary reason many soldiers go to war. He felt secure in his thoughts of home and family as he thoroughly prepared everyone—him included, for the extended period of time he would be away. His prize truck was stored, his garages and storage units were secured, the freezer was filled, and his mother was completely moved in. The Bush surge in Iraq had been going on for some time, and he hoped victory was just over the horizon.

He reflected often on the last weekend deployment gathering of family and close friends.

His father Truman, and stepmother Winnie, came to the last farewell. They spent most of their time in Florida. When they came to stay in Michigan during the summer, they stayed just a few miles from their son, on property that has been in the family for generations.

The property contained an old, one-room cabin with a small shed. No one had occupied the cabin for years. It held bad memories. When Truman and Winnie stayed on the property, they simply placed a trailer across the yard, and spent their summers on the parcel that sat around a channel connected to one of the nicer lakes in Bangor, Michigan. No one in the Hurley family would chose to stay in the cabin for even a weekend, let alone live in it. It has been ten years since Hurley even drove by the property, let alone visited it.

The small cabin contained just one large room with a table placed in the center, which served as the kitchen table, dining room, and central meeting place. Years earlier, everyone was welcome to use and enjoy the cabin. The Hurley family had enjoyed it since the late 1920s. Throughout the 1990s, the tradition continued to allow extended family and friends to enjoy the cabin.

One summer evening in June, Hurley's cousin and his two friends stayed there. The cabin overlooked a lake, which was great for bass fishing. As the three men sat around the table, finished their dinner, and relived the excitement and joy of the day, without any warning, the door burst open. Before anyone's mind could comprehend the ridiculousness of what was happening, the strange intruder—without saying anything—killed them each with a single shotgun blast to their heads.

Initially, the cousin was hit in the back of the head. The other two men, frozen in shock, were then methodically killed where they sat. It was a senseless, gruesome slaughter of three men who did nothing but enjoy their fishing trip. The friends and cousin were greatly missed, and no sense of their killing was ever made.

Some understanding came years later, when the killer was picked up in Wisconsin after being featured on the popular television show, *America's Most Wanted.* The killer was a drifter who just happened upon the cabin in Southwest Michigan before he headed west towards Chicago and Wisconsin. Hurley would never visit the property again.

***

At the command center, contact with home was through the Internet. It could be quickly and easily obtained. However, in the military war zone there were always interruptions. Whenever a U. S. soldier is killed, all outside Internet communications are shut down to prevent soldiers from communicating about a fallen comrade until the soldier's family is properly contacted. Only when the loved ones are notified are communications restored.

As can be imagined, there are frequent technical difficulties in a war zone with communications. Between family blackouts and technical difficulties, communication back home was sporadic, unreliable, and not even close to the regular contact the Hurleys hoped for. After a few weeks (which quickly became a few months), Hurley developed somewhat of a routine to: keep the power flowing, stay out of the enemies sights, and do not allow any of the million distractions to cause him to get fried by the enormous flow of electricity that he had to keep going.

Electricians in the United States are on constant alert as to the dangers of their jobs. Generator mechanics in a war zone, add a whole new meaning to the warnings associated with avoiding electrocution. Hurley and his fellow mechanics, as a priority, wanted to keep the juice flowing. They wanted to stay away from the enemy and out of the way of the Marines on their base.

Aside from the fact that this base was located in the heart of the Bloody Triangle between Bagdad and Fallujah, TQ was populated with a large number of Marines. After a few weeks, the mechanics learned that the parts of the base frequented by the Marines were the hot target zones of the enemy. In fact, after being under attack in the mess hall for the third time, it was the last time the mechanics ate there. Soon, the mechanics tried to avoid the Marines altogether, and even built their own isolated quarters away from the Marines. The mechanics moved two, old train/car-like buildings together. Over the course of a few months, they fashioned windows that could be covered with tarps to keep the sand out, and covered the roof with a rubber bladder material in an attempt to seal the cracks that were left open from the clamping system.

They lit their makeshift home with strands of Christmas lights around the walls and ceilings. It became quite a common and daily requirement to shoo out the bats that tried to share their home. The mechanics quickly learned how to fabricate their own stoves and barbeque grills. Their odd, shabby-looking building would not be as frequent of a site for attack, as was a bunker or mess hall full of Marines. Meals were prepared on hot plates within the structure, or grilled just outside the front door. Between the rubber bladder over their roof and blankets over their windows, the mechanics felt safe, secure, and at home— even with the bats.

Hurley felt comfortable with his bunk mates. Except for the regular attacks, he enjoyed the only routine that he could establish…keep the "juice" flowing. He soon learned how to establish frequent communications with Brandie back home. Being with James was like a dream come true. Brandie never imagined that a man like James would ever come into her life, and that she could be a part of a life they would build together. The dysfunctional and poor life from which she came, never could allow her to envision the possibilities that being part of the Hurley family would bring her.

The home that James built was beyond her imagination. The beauty and tranquility was beyond her dreams. Even after two years of marriage, she still could not believe it. She loved living among the wildlife. Seclusion and privacy was new to her, and something she, and her daughters, came to greatly enjoy.

Immediately after James' departure Brandie was scared and lonely. She had spent most of her life alone, and greatly enjoyed her new-found companionship. Her previous short-term, abusive relationships caused her to distrust and fear men. Thankfully, she was now healthy, and her two young daughters (the product of those brief abusive relationships), were happy and healthy too.

While James was off at war, they felt guilty for being allowed to enjoy his paradise. There was such a mixture of emotions for Brandie and the girls. They felt grateful and counted their blessings each and every day. Yet, they could not help feeling the fear from their past life; a life that lacked the safety and security that they have come to know. When was this dream going to come to an end?

Valla was of great comfort to them. She was always the reassuring shoulder to cry on, and gave Brandie and the girls the safety, and security they needed in her son's absence. It became an everyday goal of Brandie and Valla, to pray for James' safety, and take care of the needs at home in anticipation of his return.

CHAPTER 3
THE HOME FRONT & WAR ZONE

Brandie would start each day with a hot cup of coffee while watching the flowing river below. James had placed the home on a high ridge, which overlooked an expansive view of the river. The ridge slope to the river was steep, and high enough that James eventually built a set of stairways that lead from the home's back deck to a floating dock system below.

Depending on the time of year, Brandie would either enjoy her coffee outside on the gazebo, or in the home next to the picture window. Her favorite time of year was the fall, when the weather was still mild enough for her to sit in the gazebo each morning. James built a railing system around the gazebo and deck so that when the girls would awaken each morning, they were able to join Brandie, without the fear of falling down the ridge.

When James left for Iraq, it was around Christmas time in 2004. On that particular morning, she remembered how the ground was covered with snow, and the snowflakes steadily fell from the sky. Her mind wandered to the previous fall, and the annual running of the salmon. Each fall, King Salmon from Lake Michigan run the river to spawn. The Paw Paw River at the Hurley property is only about thirty feet wide, so to see a forty-inch King Salmon is spectacular. Between hunting deer and filling the freezer with salmon, the Hurley property saw much of nature's activities.

Every morning when Brandie enjoyed her coffee—regardless of the time of year—the wooded paradise surrounding her would present some wonderful contact with nature. White- tailed deer were seen every day. Turkey, rabbits, and squirrels were frequent visitors. As much as Brandie loved this homestead, it was hard to enjoy while James was off at war.

To help make sure that everyone and everything would be okay, Valla was there. She worked for the State of Michigan where she visited and helped disabled shut-ins with their home affairs. She was always trying to help others, whether through her church, or through the job that she held for more than twenty years. Living at James' place helped her financially as well. With both of their incomes, James and Valla could easily meet their living expenses.

Before leaving for Iraq, James filled the freezer with venison, turkey, rabbit, squirrel, and salmon. The freezer full of meat would last well after his return. Valla always worked a garden with James, and canned plenty of their vegetables. This part of Michigan is the fruit belt. Orchards of cherries, apples, and peaches are abundant. James always enjoyed keeping baskets of apples in his cellar that would carry him through the winter.

He had peace of mind knowing Brandie and the girls had plenty of food and supplies. With Valla moving in, and her income along with his pay, the home front was secure.

***

One day, while Valla was at work and the girls were just finishing their lunch, the quiet of the woods was broken by the barking of the Hurley Compound's guardian; a healthy black Lab named Buck. James had Buck since he was a puppy. He was now five years old. As heavenly as the place was for people, for a dog such as Buck, life could not be any better. Buck was allowed to run free. As a lab never ventures far from its owner, Buck was always around somewhere. The road was far enough away that he never ventured into harm's way. He was a protective, and loving animal.

Buck was always aware of visitors and would announce their presence well before they finished their drive up the long winding driveway. Brandie was curious as to the visitor this day, since no one has been by since James had left to serve overseas. Her curiosity and concern peaked when she saw the four-door sedan driven by a man in his 30s. Buck kept a watchful eye as the man approached the front door and extended a greeting to Brandie through the screen door. He identified himself as Brian Adams, a realtor with Sun Downers Realty. James had been gone now for a few months, and they were settled into a routine. James had not told Brandie to expect any guests or visitors while he was gone, so she felt the stranger had wandered to their place by mistake.

***

At the same time in Iraq, Hurley was not necessarily settling into a routine. He felt comfortable with the men he worked with. There was a clear sense of camaraderie and trust you would expect and envision in the U. S. Military. He was surprised by the diversity of age among the soldiers. There becomes quite a diverse group of soldiers when guard units mesh with full-time combat personnel. While serving in the National Guard for twenty-five years, Hurley never saw himself as just a weekend warrior.

There is an interesting dynamic between a soldier in his early 20s in his first year in the service, and a man like Hurley who was pushing 45, and whose mission was to keep the "juice" flowing. They each had to rely on the other, work for the safety of the other, and strive for the same objectives. It was a classic example of men of different experiences and vocations coming together in war; Citizen Soldiers meshed with combat personnel.

Communications between Hurley and his wife was always pleasant. It allowed him to take a mental break, and for a few moments in his mind, go home. Brandie appreciated the opportunity to learn that he was safe. When they spoke, he didn't talk about the war. Just to hear his voice provided a sense of security—no matter how false it was.

By just hearing his voice, she could, for those moments, know that everything was okay.

He loved to hear about how the girls went on daily hikes throughout the property and the great adventures they would have. The Michigan wilderness can be exhilarating. There were no bears or wolves in this part of Michigan, unlike the northern part of the state. While there were coyotes and some dangerous snakes, they would be of no harm to the family's own private nature preserve.

Communication blackouts came with more frequency as the Bush surge progressed. The couple made a rule to send regular emails and verbal communications every few weeks between blackouts. Disruptions of lines, blackouts, or other issues, made a regular schedule unnecessary and confusing.

Other than missing their soldier, the women and girls on the Hurley homestead had it pretty nice and easy. The place was in good order, and with Valla's income and his military pay, the daily concerns of getting by was not an issue. Their only financial debt was the mortgage. Their balance was around $100,000. They were living a comfortable, middle-class life. Hurley just wanted his tour to be over.

Dreams of the next deer hunt or finishing his 62' Chevy would sometimes come to him in his sleep. Most of the time, his thoughts and sleep moments were spent concentrating on his war efforts. The surge was meant to be the opportunity for a defining moment for the Bush presidency. It was the Bush Administration's opportunity to take control of this war and lead us to victory. Hurley felt really good about his mom living with Brandie and the girls. Part of what allowed him to function and excel in performing his war duties, was the peace he felt knowing his family was safe back home. The home front was his mental escape, and gave him a sense of security.

***

Brandie met Brian Adams, the realtor with Sun Downer's Realty with a smile and apprehension. She thought, *what in the world would a*

realtor be doing on James Hurley's doorstep? Her initial feeling that he must have wandered off quickly dissipated as he asked, "to whom he could speak with concerning the Hurley property?" If this smiling, friendly sort of guy knew how much James loves this property, he would have known not to even step foot on it, let alone drive up with his apparent thoughts and motives.

A scared rush overwhelmed Brandie, and she blurted that no, the Hurleys had no use for a realtor. This property, and all of its buildings, belonged to James Hurley. James built everything here with his blood, sweat, and tears, and he planned on living there until the day he died. What could possibly possess a realtor to come soliciting while the owner was away at war for our country? It was all quite surreal. She could not imagine where James was, or what he was going through. She did know that she needed him now more than ever.

Brian Adams explained that he would be happy to list the Hurley property and find a buyer that would pay more money than what was owed. Brandie's first thought was, *This guy must be horribly mistaken.* He was simply not making any sense, and his proposal of selling James' property while he was at war was absurd. Brandie made it clear that there was no interest to sell and explained how the entire family loved it here; he was surely crazy for even thinking otherwise. To her, the whole idea was exacerbated, given that James was in Iraq.

She knew her husband loved this property and would never sell it. Brandie instructed Adams that he should leave immediately. He should consider it a mistake, but please never come back. As Adams drove away down the driveway, Brandie thought that it was odd. *How was it that Adams spoke of such particulars of James' name and the property? Perhaps it was some scam run on families at war.* Nevertheless, she dismissed Adams' visit shortly after Buck escorted him off the property.

That evening, after Valla's return home from work, the four sat down to a nice home-cooked meal. Typically, Brandie would have spent much of the day in meal preparations for Valla's return from work, and the girls' evening dinner. All of the Hurley women enjoyed mealtime together as a family, and were growing especially close given the need, and reliance upon one another and their shared loss of having James away at war.

Brandie, never having had an unknown visitor to the property before, shared the peculiar experience with Valla that evening over a dinner of Valla's favorites of chipped squirrel, mashed potatoes and gravy, and carrots from the family garden. The women laughed at how preposterous the idea of selling the property was. Just thinking about such an event (let alone the idea that James wasn't there because he was at war) was just ludicrous.

Why would they sell? What is a short sale? Brian Adams kept stating this term that Brandie never heard before. He said that it was to their benefit to engage in a short sale at this time. Clearly, this must have been some type of scam. It simply made no sense.

CHAPTER
THE TWILIGHT ZONE

Up until a week or so after the visit from the realtor, Brandie had completely dismissed his visit. Then, one day, during her morning gazebo coffee ritual, a sedan drove up the driveway. At first she didn't recognize the driver. But when he got out of the car and removed his hat, she recognized him as the realtor from a couple of weeks ago. This time, there wasn't even an inquiry about selling, just a quick request as to whether Brandie had given any thought to the short-sale idea he had previously proposed.

Short sale? Not knowing what the heck that was, or what he meant by that, Brandie clearly wanted to understand if this guy had the wrong property, or if he was some type of scam artist. Clearly, a second visit required her to be proactive in protecting the family and their property. She wanted clear identification and verification as to why he was there.

Brian Adams reintroduced himself, and explained that he was hired by a mortgage servicing company to help people going through financial difficulties, avoid foreclosures. He explained that if someone sells their property and pays off the mortgage, they could avoid the expense and hardship associated with a foreclosure.

Brandie told Brian that he was mistaken. She explained that James had never missed a mortgage payment in more than ten years, and that he loved this home, and would never sell it. Despite her mild protest, Brian left his card, and told her that she needed to let him know what they want to do with the property. Brandie repeatedly told him that James was in the United States Army, serving in Iraq. Brian told her that it is not an issue for him, but that James, Valla, and she, needed to follow up on the mortgage status and get back to him so he could help them find a buyer.

CHAPTER

LINCOLN

The exchange between Brandie and Brian is exactly what Abraham Lincoln did not want for his Civil War Soldiers 150 years ago.Lincoln felt that while one of his soldiers was off fighting in a war for their country, their concentration should be entirely on their war efforts. Lincoln was behind legislation that protected his soldiers from creditors while they were at war. These efforts would allow for credit situations to be "frozen," until the soldier was allowed to come home and deal with the debt issues, rather than trying to stay alive and negotiate on a legal issue back home.

Congress enacted the Soldiers' and Sailors' Civil Relief Act (SSCRA) in 1918. It echoed Lincoln's sentiment and intent. In 2003, Congress updated and amended the protections as the United States was entering the war in Iraq. At that time, Colonels John S. Odom Jr. and Gregory Huckabee were assigned to the Pentagon. General William Howard Taft IV (President Taft's great grandson) assigned the two colonels the task to make the necessary updates to the Soldiers' and Sailors' Civil Relief Act. The driving force to this update was the upcoming war, and the outdated monetary thresholds contained in the eighty-five-year-old SSCRA.

In 1918, some of the U.S. military branches did not exist. While updates were being made, it was obviously the opportune time for the congressional amendments to reflect a new name for the Act. Colonel Huckabee had a conference with a room full of colonels from each branch. They pondered the new name. Of course the Air Force colonel thought it should be the Air Force, Soldiers, Sailor's, Marine's and Coast Guard Act. On and on the exchange of new names went with each branch putting itself first. It was through this debate that Colonel Huckabee chose the name, The Servicemembers Civil Relief Act (SCRA).

While the name changed, the mission did not. In fact, it expanded to include the new branches of military. Hurley's active duty service with the National Guard would be included in this act. Therefore, upon Sgt. James Hurley's active duty status, a non-judicial foreclosure action could not be brought against him. While he served in Iraq, his home, and his family's safety, was suppose to be protected.

Even if he had defaulted on the mortgage—which he clearly did not—a mortgage holder can only seek a judicial action against him in regards to foreclosure. The SCRA is clear that a non-judicial proceeding cannot commence against a soldier while on active duty. Even if the mortgage holder sought a judicial foreclosure action against Hurley, the SCRA protected him from participating in the judicial proceedings while thousands of miles away in a foreign country at war.

By not seeking a judicial action, Hurley was denied the opportunity to defend himself. Legally, once he came home, the bank could then proceed against him for any failure to fulfill the mortgage terms. Interest would continue to accrue, and the bank's rights would always be fully protected and in priority. Even perhaps without the hyperactive nature of the foreclosure crisis, the bank would have learned of its error, and that fact that no default existed.

Time means nothing as far as a loss to the bank in this situation. The old adage that "time is money", works for the banks as they continue to earn its interest and late fees. Just as Lincoln envisioned, there is no harm to the financial institution. The soldier is not getting a hand out, as they are required to fully comply with their financial obligations. At the same time, they are simply allowed the opportunity to put forth their entire energy toward their war effort.

The day after Brian Adams' last visit, the Hurley family received a notice from a mortgage servicing company that there was a payment deficiency with Deutsche Bank. Valla found the name of the bank to be foreign to her, as she had never heard of it before. Sometime after her son obtained his mortgage, it was sold to another bank. Many financial institutions purchase what are perceived to be high-risk loans that belong to military personnel. The high-risk loan provided the financial institution with an opportunity to charge a higher interest rate, and the potential to earn high returns on the collection of late fees.

Whenever a guard unit is activated, there are various legal discussions that will allow them to take care of their financial concerns while they are away. The soldiers are given forms to send to creditors, to inform them of their active duty status, as well as the rights and protections afforded by the SCRA. Many soldiers arrange for automatic withdrawals from their military pay to satisfy mortgage obligations, and notify unsecured creditors (i.e., credit card companies) of the maximum six percent interest rate they can be charged while on active duty according to the SCRA.

To further validate a soldier's claim, the United States Department of Defense operates a website for financial institutions to check on a debtor's military status. The Defense Manpower Data Center has a database and process that takes no more than fifteen seconds to check the status of military personnel. Brandie and Valla sat at the kitchen table at a loss as to what this foreclosure notice meant. They remembered discussions with James that the payments would be automatically taken from his military pay once he was in Iraq. While James was in California for two months of training, Valla helped her son coordinate the payments.

Between his last paycheck with the Cheese Factory, and the months between the activation of his military pay, the Hurley family did have a brief financial crisis. After his return from California, money was tight. The family had gone a month without James' paycheck. Fortunately, Valla's paycheck and financial contribution helped immensely.

She was sure that she never missed a mortgage payment. There may have been one that was late, but never missed.

Other than paying creditors, most of the Hurley money was spent on getting the necessary provisions for Iraq. Between his training in California, and what he was hearing from returning veteran mechanics, Hurley spent more than $1,000 to supplement his military-issued toolbox. Valla spent more than $500 on extra socks, underwear, medical and dental care products, and other incidentals that she wanted her son to have while he was away at war.

Brandie and Valla agreed that there must have been some type of error. They would notify the mortgage servicing company that all the payments were made, and soon there would be an automatic withdrawal process in place from James' military pay. They both agreed in an almost unspoken manner that at this time, James did not need to be bothered about the visit from Brian Adams or the bank letter. They both felt it was an easy error to be reconciled.

Valla pulled James' files and called the mortgage servicing company to dispute the company's position. In addition to confirming the mortgage was up to date, she re-confirmed that her son had filled out, and sent all of the paperwork the guard unit gave him to notify creditors of his deployment. Valla forced the mortgage-servicing representative to be responsive to her position, and was confident that this matter was closed.

***

A few weeks went by and it seemed that everyone was falling into a good routine again. Valla went to work about forty hours per week with weekends off. Brandie kept the house in order and prepared most of the meals. The girls were thriving in the home.

One evening, Valla came home from work and found Brandie crying in the gazebo. She was accustomed to seeing Brandie in the gazebo in the morning, but not at night, and certainly not crying. The two had become quite close and Valla's maternal feelings made her wonder if

James was okay. It was a great sense of relief that Brandie's big upset was over a letter from the bank.

Valla knew that the home was fine. She felt that big banks make mistakes, and like a big computer loop, once you were in, it was impossible to break out. But this time, she was going to put an end to this nonsense.

The fact that she thought that his mortgage was current was irrelevant. The bank was not allowed to foreclose or call the loan while her son was on active duty. Valla sent military documentation to the bank and the mortgage servicing company. When James called, he reassured his mother that everything would be okay. There was an officer in his unit that was suppose to help the soldiers with anything that might come up at home and that he would go and talk with him about what to do.

Hurley was reassured by his home-front officer, not to worry about any of this. He told him that he could not be foreclosed on while away at war. In fact, the officer in Iraq sent him to a Judge Advocate General (JAG) officer in Iraq. This attorney assured him that he should focus his energies on his war effort, and that the SCRA would protect his home. To give Hurley further peace of mind, the JAG officer and Hurley coordinated with the Post Commander's office back in Michigan to fax his active duty order to the bank and the mortgage servicing company.

**

A few weeks after Valla was sure that the issues had been resolved, she was now feeling frightened that there may be some serious problems. She came home one evening to find a note attached to the front door from the attorneys for the mortgage servicing company and the bank. It read that the Hurley property was being foreclosed on. The notice indicated that, under Michigan law, the property was subject to a non-judicial foreclosure and that the home would be sold through public auction on the courthouse steps within the next thirty days.

While Valla thought that this was simply ridiculous, she was very scared. Her fear and tension was alleviated as her son told her not to worry. He explained that he again went to see a JAG officer and was told to not worry. Just to be sure, Valla drove to the corner gas station in town to fax another set of documents about her son's active duty to the bank's attorneys. After the latest round of notices, Brandie and Valla felt confident that the message was clear. Not only did they convey the military orders, her son's guard unit commanding officer sent the military orders that verified the unit's active military status.

While Valla and Brandie felt confident that the message was received and now everything would be okay, there was a notarized signature indicating that the Mortgagee/James Hurley was not in the military. Specifically, on the non-military affidavit, it was stated:

The undersigned, being first duly sworn, states that upon investigation he is informed and believes that none of the persons named in the notice attached to the sheriff's deed of mortgage foreclosure, nor any person upon whom they or any of them were dependent, were in the military service of the United States at the time of sale or for six months prior thereto; nor the present grantee(s). The undersigned further states that this affidavit is made for the purpose of preserving a record and clearing title by virtue of the Solders' and Sailors' Relief Act of 1940, as amended.

Valla surmised that there must have been some kind of mistake on the bank and mortgage servicing company's part concerning James' status. And, that the affidavit that declared James was not in the military service would prove to be their error.

Obviously, James was on active duty in Iraq. To make matters worse, the bank was now refusing to accept any mortgage payments. Valla thought the computer loop could be broken and the mistake fixed, now that attorneys that represent the bank and mortgage-servicing company were involved .

For the next month, Valla, Brandie, and the girls' lives went on in a peaceful and simple way. It had been more than five months since the payment issues occurred while James was in California. And it seemed, with the apparent error on the sworn affidavit and non-judicial foreclosure paperwork, all worries relating to the mortgage issue were behind them.

They all greatly missed James and worried for his safety. The winter months would soon be behind them. The winter always seemed so isolating given how much the outdoors are enjoyed during the other three seasons. In the fall, the Hurley property is alive with salmon fishing, and deer and turkey hunting. Spring brings a rejuvenation of life back from the cold winters. Michigan sees the return of the spring Robins and all the other birds.

Brandie and the girls enjoyed morel mushroom hunting. It seemed like a daily and endless Easter Egg Hunt as they looked for mushrooms (a favorite activity for many Michiganders). Many children troop through the woods making up mushroom songs as they seemingly pull the magic morsels to the surface. Many a morel hunter declares the finding of a mushroom in a spot that just moments earlier seemed bare.

Summer for the Hurleys meant lying by the river where they soaked up the hot sun and enjoyed the cool running river. James loved to canoe and kayak as much as he loved to jump in the water and going for a cool, relaxing swim. Fishing rods always had wet lines. From the fall salmon run to the January steelhead, summer was a time anything was possible. Northern Pike, Bluegill or Rainbow Trout (the Paw Paw River is a fisherman's utopia), and the Hurleys enjoyed it like the river deserved.

Brandie and James had regular contact through e-mail and occasional phone conversations, which were greatly enjoyed. James loved to hear about the girls' latest hiking adventures and exploration of the Hurley wilderness. Brandie and the girls were personalizing the property. The big Maple tree behind James' workshop, that was so perfect for climbing, was known as Magical. The high ridge cutting between the river and the creek was Wolf Mountain. The open expanse behind Wolf Mountain was the Hurley Serengeti. There was a true love and enjoyment of the land and James never grew bored of listening to Brandie tell the latest tale of adventure.

Valla enjoyed being a part of Brandie and the girls' lives. She enjoyed seeing how much they enjoyed life. There was a growing mutual love and respect among the four. Valla had the daily routine and grind that came with a full time job. Fortunately, Valla is a nurturer and found much reward providing care to her clients. Every day she would visit a disabled shut in and help them with a wide variety of tasks.

From the mundane running of a fresh vacuum sweeper to a heart-felt wound care assistant, Valla was a women deserving of much love and admiration. She raised James with honor and respect, and required nothing more from him. She was a stout, fit, strawberry blonde fire-cracker with blue green eyes. She had a penchant for saying what she thought—only after careful and thoughtful deliberation. James shared many of her physical characteristics from the hair and eye color to the personality traits of giving others care and respect. He was a true man of honor.

James fell for Brandie at a Halloween party. After being married to her for two years, there was no question he would open his mind and heart to loving the two little girls. Just before the activation order rumor started flying around, James and Brandie planned for James to adopt Jacqueline, 4, and Autumn, 2.

After James was in Iraq, he reminded Brandie that it is on her to-do list to have everything in order for them to finalize the adoptions when he gets back. Nothing could have comforted Brandie more.

Everything was moving along as best as could be expected for the Hurleys, given a love one was at war on the other side of the planet. Bush's surge was heating up Iraq. Fighting, blood shed, and death was a daily occurrence in Iraq, and the triangular location of the cities, towns, and enclaves was the hot spot. Hurley kept the juice flowing through many intense moments and days without any sleep or rest. For him, it seemed that the intensity rarely gave up or subsided.

Brandie and the girls welcomed the blooming daisies, daffodils and tulips. The warming sun was invigorating from the winter darkness. One beautiful spring morning after Brandie's ritual of enjoying a cup of coffee in the gazebo, the three made tiaras and gowns woven from flowers. They were queens of the flower gardens who ruled the flowers. Squirrels and chipmunks were in for a spectacular pageantry by the Hurley girls.

Just as the three thought of making a bouquet of flowers for the kitchen table to greet Valla with her dinner, they heard a vehicle come up the driveway. The girls just sat in the fresh grass as an elderly rotund, kind-looking gentleman identified himself as "Walt," a court officer. He inquired as to the whereabouts of James Hurley. Brandie informed him that James was in Iraq.

"Really?" Walt said in an unbelieving tone and manner of disrespect. "Well, what is he doing there?"

Brandie, almost ignorant to the man's sarcasm, said, "James is a sergeant in the United States Military fighting in our country's war effort."

"Well, consider yourself served, and have a good day." With that, Walt turned and departed as quickly as he appeared.

Brandie quickly gathered up the girls and went into the house where she laid the paperwork on the kitchen table. Valla would not be greeted with a bouquet of flowers this evening. And her dinner would be ruined with the paperwork that indicated that the Hurleys were now being evicted from their home.

CHAPTER 6

NON-JUDICIAL FORECLOSURES & EVICTIONS

President Lincoln, and every president since, has wanted U.S. soldiers to have the ability to focus their energy and attention on their war efforts. It is equally important that their mothers, wives, and relatives are not conducting business affairs for them while they serve their country. While Valla and Brandie seemed to have conducted James' affairs in good order, how could they now be served with eviction papers? The paperwork that sat on the Hurley kitchen table indicated that the owner of the property was now the bank. They had conducted the non-judicial foreclosure and were seeking their eviction.

Non-judicial foreclosures and evictions in Michigan are known as proceedings that are summary in nature; meaning the attorneys that represent a party have to follow certain legal steps to establish how the matter proceeds through court. It summarily flows through the court system from the initial filings through the court's final judgment. Summary proceedings are simplified procedures for recovery of real property.

The judge in particular heavily relies on the attorney's adherence to the rules and requirements. Attorneys are officers of the court. As officers of the court, they are bound by the rules and procedures that must be strictly followed. A non-judicial foreclosure in Michigan does not involve the court system or judge at all; it is non-judicial. The party seeking the foreclosure must adhere to the established requirements to perfect the process.

The act of seeking a non-judicial foreclosure against someone who is on active duty in the United States Military is prohibited. The SCRA is clear and precise on this issue. In non-judicial foreclosure proceedings, there is a requirement of the non-military affidavit, stating that (under oath) the person in which this action is commenced against is not in the military. Such a declaration is also necessary before an eviction is commenced.

Contrary to the SCRA and what Hurley was told by the JAG Officers and Guard units (and everything Valla and Brandie were told by the military advisors at the Michigan State Capitol in Lansing), a soldier on active duty can be non-judicially foreclosed upon *if* someone is willing to go forward with the process in a manner that does not comply with Federal law. The non-judicial foreclosure was illegal. Once someone obtains a foreclosure, then the property needs to be sold or possessed. If someone is occupying the property (like Valla, Brandie, and the girls), there needs to be an eviction.

The SCRA is a strong and powerful protection for our soldiers. Throughout U.S. history its terms and requirements have seen massive voluntary compliance. Case filings in which a party seeks compensation from military personnel in an effort to violate the SCRA are rare. There has only been one jury seated to hear a case that alleged a non-judicial foreclosure that violated a soldier's SCRA rights…and Hurley would soon become the key plaintiff for that landmark case.

Generally, financial institutions in the United States have polices and procedures in place to ensure compliance with the SCRA. In addition, attorneys (as officers of the court) do not engage in behavior that disregard legal requirements, and work in direct contravention of the law. The Hurley case is the example of what happens when banks and their attorneys violate the SCRA.

An eviction of a soldier on active duty is strictly controlled by the SCRA. Upon the commencement of an eviction, the pleadings declare, "for a defendant on active military duty, default judgment shall not be entered except as provided by the Servicemembers Civil Relief Act."

If a soldier on active duty is facing an eviction, special precautions are taken. First, the party seeking the eviction must make the judge aware of the active duty status. The court then determines whether the individual's active duty status affects their ability to defend the cause of action. Sometimes the judge will even appoint an attorney for the soldier to aid in the determination of this issue.

The attorney who sought James Hurley's eviction did not advise the court of Hurley's active duty status. Quite to the contrary, the court documents commenced against Hurley state that, "Plaintiff was mortgagee, defendant was mortgagor. Plaintiff foreclosed defendant's mortgage and was the successful bidder at sale. The redemption period has expired, defendant failed to redeem and refuses to vacate." Furthermore, attached to the Complaint for Termination of Tenancy, the attorney attached a copy of the Non-Military Affidavit, which stated:

"The undersigned, being first duly sworn, states that upon investigation he is informed and believes that none of the persons named in the notice attached to the sheriff's deed or mortgage foreclosure, nor any person upon whom they or any of them were dependent, were in the military service of the United States at the time of sale or for six months prior thereto; nor the present grantee(s).

As a result of the awkwardness felt by the process server who left the documents with Brandie, the process server said something to the judge about Hurley's military status. The older rotund scruffy man (Walt) who frightened Brandie with papers for eviction was actually a kind gentleman with a heart of gold. One day while passing the judge in the courthouse hallway, Walt mentioned the eviction paperwork that he had recently served. He wrote on the return of service (that gets filed with the court) a brief statement about the Defendant being in the military in Iraq. To him, it was a one of a kind exchange that he had with the wife of a comrade.

Being prior military himself, he just knew something did not seem right. He was following the war in Iraq and was aware of the U.S. surge. The least he could do was to write the note on the return of service, and when he had the opportunity, point it out to the judge. A summary proceeding eviction is really set up as a process of filing forms in the proper order. For the most part, the judge who conducts evictions is an administrator who assures the accuracy of the forms, and compliance with the proceedings of the Michigan Landlord Tenant Act. The issue of service is crucial for the commencement of the hoop-jumping process. Also of vital importance to any action, is the accuracy of the non-military affidavit.

CHAPTER 7
HURLEY'S EVICTION

Judge Clarke sat in his chambers to review the pleadings for the next week's evictions. He recalled his recent conversation with Walt, and was interested in seeing the return of service. For a couple of weeks, he had kept a careful lookout for what Walt said he wrote on the return of service. Sure enough, there it was in the Hurley file: "according to spouse, Hurley is in the military in Iraq." Oddly, Judge Clarke noticed that the attorneys for the bank had already filed the paperwork for final judgment.

The paperwork filed was the type that would typically be expected in a case being uncontested with a party being evicted. Many times the tenant may have moved, and the landlord was merely filing what was technically necessary in order to comply with the Landlord Tenant Act. Judge Clarke interpreted the Hurley pleadings to be the case where the tenant had no interest in contesting the eviction.

Based on Walt's notes, Judge Clarke scheduled a hearing before he would grant the bank's default against James Hurley. While he was aware that Walt was told that Hurley was in Iraq, the bank's paperwork said that he was not in the United States Military on active duty. Further, Judge Clarke thought that even if Hurley was in Iraq, there was a chance he may *not* have any interest in continuing to stay at this property.

After the judge was told that there seemed to be people living on the premises, he felt that maybe if there was an interest on Hurley's part, someone in the home could shed some light on the matter. Again, it was not necessarily clear through the paperwork the bank filed, that Hurley had owned the property. The Judge was thinking that just because Hurley was in Iraq, he might not want this property. If there were any interests, the judge would defer to Hurley's desires. Erring to the benefit of the soldier, a tenant would not harm a landlord under these circumstances. In the same regard, to allow an eviction of a soldier with no history or interest in the real estate, would not cause any harm. Such a thought process on the judge's part relied entirely on the absence of fraud in the pleadings. Having a hearing prevents something bad from happening, if the pleadings contain fraud. Judge Clarke was just not prepared for, nor had he contemplated what was about to happen to the Hurleys.

The actions of Walt on the day of service by no means intended to scare Brandie. However, it became apparent to her that the man wanting to see James, did not believe her, or simply did not care what she said about his military service. She recalled that, after he had the verbal exchange with her, that he made a few notations on the papers that he was holding. He handed a set to Brandie, kept another set, and told her that she and whoever else was living there needed to move. And, that she should give James a copy and advise him accordingly. It was when Brandie reiterated to him that James was in Iraq that he turned to walk away.

After placing the papers on the kitchen table, the word eviction rushed through her body and made her feel numb. They had to move or be forcibly removed. She was overwhelmed with fear and memories from the past. The last two years were the longest she ever lived in one place. But more urgent was the sickness she felt for James. This place was part of him. He built most of what was there. Again, all she could think about was that he hadn't missed a payment for ten years, and now he was going to be forcibly removed—all while he was in Iraq. He was on the other side of the planet and unable to do anything about this…and wasn't even aware of it.

Valla and Brandie reviewed and scoured the eviction papers in disbelief. In the boldest and largest print, it stated: "Plaintiff was mortgagee, defendant was mortgagor. Plaintiff foreclosed defendant's mortgage and was the successful bidder at sale. The redemption period has expired, defendant failed to redeem and refuses to vacate." This had all been straightened out. James is in Iraq; he is on active duty. No payments have been missed. The nightmare just continued. Everyone—the bank, the mortgage servicing company, and their attorneys—was aware that it had all been a mistake. Obviously, the error just kept growing. There seemed to be a clear understanding on the part of the bank's attorneys that James was in Iraq and on active duty.

Valla was resolved to go to the eviction hearing at the courthouse in South Haven set for the following week. She was anxious to see the judge and clear up this horrible mistake once and for all. That evening, Brandie discussed the eviction papers with James, who was full of questions; none of which Brandie could answer. He could only repeat what his JAG officers told him: "Don't worry, they cannot do this to you while you are here. You can resolve it when you get home."

"How do you get evicted from your own home?" the two of them echoed back and forth. The eviction papers listed the bank as the Plaintiff and James Hurley and all other occupants as the Tenant. The foreclosure must have gone through and transferred title to the bank. But how?

James encouraged Valla to go to the hearing. Clearly, he could not be there. It all seemed quite simple anyway. It was a mistake. He would go see the JAG officer again.

The South Haven Courthouse is located along the shores of Lake Michigan. It is a satellite court, which serves the western part of Van Buren County. The Hurley eviction was scheduled for a status conference, and hearing for default before Judge Clarke. Judge Clarke rescheduled the matter for a status conference in chambers so that he could determine if there was any party that had an interest in the premises. Specifically, Judge Clarke wanted to see if anyone would appear and express an interest on behalf of James Hurley.

On the morning of the status conference, Valla arrived at 8:30 a.m., just as the courthouse was opening. She was ready to meet with the judge and get this matter right once and for all. Her son was away at war. The least she could do was protect the home that he loved so much and worked so hard to obtain and develop. The main doors of the South Haven Courthouse open into a small informal rotunda. On one end of the room are the doors to the courtroom. To the right are sets of chairs near windows that overlook the parking lot. Left of the entrance is a hallway along which are open window areas to the clerk's office. Upon entering the building, Valla went to the first clerk's window and was instructed to have a seat in the main rotunda area.

She felt very confident in her position. The JAG officers told her son that this could not be done to him while he was in Iraq. Everyone from the bank, the mortgage servicing company, and attorneys all knew James was on active duty. The Guard representatives at the State Capitol and at Fort Custer assured her that military laws protected the home; after all, they provided all of the needed documentation.

When Valla asked about whether she should hire an attorney, the representative's response was "Why? It is illegal for them to proceed against James; it simply cannot be done." Now she was in a position to talk with the judge and finally put a stop to this nightmare. She was not going to leave this courthouse until she knew that it was finally over and James' home was safe.

By 9 a.m., the rotunda was full of people. It was a cross section of the community. Some sat, some paced, and lawyers in suits came and went from the clerk's office to the rotunda, and to the courtroom. An elderly gentlemen in a sweater vest and suit jacket, walked into the middle of the rotunda and shouted out, "Hurley!" Valla was initially set aback. She did not expect this type of announcement, and it was odd to hear her name in a courthouse for the first time in her life. At first, she didn't know what to do. So, as if back in grade school, she raised her hand.

The man looked at her, and she rose and approached him. With a cracked smile, he confirmed that she was there for James Hurley. Upon her confirmation, he told her to follow him. The two walked through the rotunda and past the clerk's windows. They approached a door marked "For Courthouse Personnel Only." They stood there momentarily until a buzz and clicking sound caused the man to grab the door and push it open. Valla followed, not knowing where they were going.

They continued through the door and down a long hallway. They went into a room with a large conference table with chairs. As they entered the room, the man introduced himself as Whitney Blalock; he was here on behalf of the bank. The elderly gentleman sat at the head of the table and gestured for Valla to sit to his immediate right. As they entered the room, Blalock slammed the door behind them louder than he anticipated. It startled Valla and immediately put her in a scared and defensive mode. When he instructed her to sit to his right, she immediately complied with his command and sat there, quiet and stoic. He pulled out a thin file from his briefcase and with a penetrating look in his blue-grey eyes asked, "Why have you not moved out of the property?"

"Because it's my son's house," she shot back.

The man pierced his lips and nodded his head ever so slightly as if he were mockingly repeating what he just said.

"My son is at war in Iraq. He is on active duty in the United States Military. This is his home. You cannot do this," Valla said.

Blalock simply continued to stare at her and nod his head as if continuing the repetition of his earlier question, "Why have you not moved out of the property yet?"

Valla broke the silence by stating that the Guard and the JAG told the bank and their lawyers of her son's military status. "Everyone knows that James is in Iraq and you cannot do this."

At this, the man's head stopped nodding; but, his squinting eyes opened and his mouth now more relaxed like he was about to say something.

Valla shot out, "James has never missed a payment in over ten years. We are paid to date on this loan. He has been paying on the property for over ten years."

Valla felt so refreshed that she was able to say face to face what she had been wanting to for so long.

Blalock sat back in his chair and smiled. Without taking his eyes off of her he said, "I'm sorry, but you have to get out."

Valla was in shock. "What do you mean?"

"You have to leave the property."

Valla was about to lose it. She simply responded, "I want to see the judge. Who are you?"

"I told you," he said. "I represent the bank. They own the house now."

Valla thought, *I'm done with this guy. He is an idiot.* "You cannot do this to us, James is in Iraq. I want to see the judge!"

Shrugging his shoulders Blalock said, "Fine, I will go see the judge and see if he will allow us some time today for you to tell him whatever it is you want to say."

He got up and told Valla to follow him back out to the courthouse rotunda. The room was still packed with people. The room seemed full, noisy, and in a high spin. She just wanted to forget the exchange she just had with this man. She felt that she was visibly shaking, but needed to hold it together to see the judge. She was not afraid, she was mad. How did this man not accept what she was telling him?

Blalock walked back to the judge's chambers. The South Haven Courthouse is a very casual environment for lawyers. They freely walk around the outer office chambers, helping themselves to coffee or whatever baked goods may be on the coffee table. Lawyers walk in and out of the chambers to see the judge when he is available. When Blalock walked into the chambers, there were four other lawyers seemingly lounging around the chambers with the judge, who was behind his desk. It was like a family room with a bunch of friends who were there just sitting around, visiting, and chitchatting about South Haven's upcoming high school game.

Blalock silently sat on a couch across the room. The assistant prosecutor and defense attorney sat in the chairs in front of the judge's desk. As the chitchat subsided, they reported to the judge that they were able to work out a plea deal. Passing over the others, the judge focused on Blalock and asked, "Well, what do you have on Hurley?"

"Nothing really," responded Blalock.

"Well...", the judge cut him off, "I know James Hurley is probably not here, right? But did anyone show up on his behalf?"

Blalock casually responded, "Not really. Just some folks that have taken over living at the house while he is gone. I have told them they have to leave. Instead of two weeks, we would be willing to give them thirty days to get out."

The judge shook his head and asked Blalock if they needed to go into the courtroom to put anything on the record. Blalock responded that he didn't think so, as they understood the issues and were in agreement.

At this point, the judge looked directly at Blalock and asked him if they seemed acceptable to that? Blalock shook his head in agreement.

"Well, since no one from Hurley has expressed an interest in the property, I will give you your order. However, I will not issue a Writ for Possession until two weeks after the thirty days, if they have not yet left."

Blalock rose to his feet, "Thank you, your Honor." he then left the room.

Judge Clarke felt comfortable with the exchange as he gave the parties what he thought they agreed. Essentially, the parties agreed to what the bank's pleadings state, and what would be reflected in the final order. In addition, in the final judgment, there is specific language related to the SCRA that included: "For a defendant on active military duty, default judgment shall not be entered except as provided by the Servicemembers' Civil Relief Act."

Blalock returned to Valla and told her that the judge was not able to hear the case. He said the judge stated that they could adjourn today's hearing, and come back in forty-five days for a full hearing on whatever she wanted to personally say to the judge.

Valla's heart sank. She needed this to be over. They needed to stop harassing her and her son.

She asked, "Don't you understand? Why do we have to come back? James is on active duty, he is in Iraq, and this is his home."

"I'm sorry. I don't know. I am just here for the bank and they need you to leave. Maybe you are right and this can all be worked out later. I am not with the bank, I was just asked to come here today. Sometimes they call me to help cover things for them. I will pass on what you have said. You can tell the judge your story when we come back."

Blalock's words were calming, yet confusing to Valla. She left the courthouse that day believing that they were okay. According to Blalock, she would have the opportunity to talk directly with the judge later. That evening, Valla shared the good news with James that she would be able to see the judge next month. She stopped the eviction. It was important for Valla to keep James' spirits up. She was scared for her son in Iraq and he did not need to worry about them and the home.

***

By now, Hurley was developing relationships with his fellow soldiers. Words cannot express or describe the bonding that occurs among soldiers at war, and he developed several such relationships with his unit comrades. He was happy to hear what his mom had to say. Her words made sense, given what the JAG officer in Iraq told him to do—focus on his war efforts. What he had been told appeared to be true. They could not take his home while he was in Iraq. Besides, he could not understand how there could be a problem since he has made all of his payments for the past ten years.

It was good to hear his mom's voice. He longed for home, but he had to focus on his war efforts. He was in a very dangerous part of Iraq. Communication blackouts were occurring every week and he had many close calls with being electrocuted as he crawled around like a mouse in the massive generators. Aside from the frequent enemy attacks on the base, electricity was his own hidden danger as he had to keep it flowing for the command center and the hospital.

CHAPTER
COMMUNICATIONS

It had been a while since Valla had gone to court, or had spoken with James. Every time they tried to contact him, the lines of communication were blacked out. The entire family knew what a communication blackout meant, and it caused everyone to be put into a somber mood. They had almost come to prefer James not contacting them, so they would not be a distraction to him. As much as they liked to hear that he was okay, it almost seemed more soothing to know that he was staying safe and focused.

Valla's mental calendar seemed to be calling to her. She felt she should be hearing from the court soon. That morning, she enjoyed a coffee with Brandie in her coffee spot on the gazebo. The morning chill quickly left with the warmth from the rising sun. Just as they were feeling the day would be a good day, they both noticed the sound, then sight of an approaching vehicle coming up the driveway. Buck the dog, was still inside.

The quietness of the morning was broken by the sound of the dark four-door sedan on the gravel driveway. Their stomachs sank as a black sheriff's car approached the gazebo. The uniformed officer approached the women without a sound. As he came to the gazebo, Valla and Brandie simultaneously rose to their feet as he inquired if they lived there.

"Yes," they responded.

"Are you the Hurleys?" he inquired.

"Yes," they answered. Each flashed to visions of James in their minds and feared the worse for what the man was about to say. Both ladies then blurted out, "Is James okay?"

The deputy stood still and calmly said, "I'm sorry to have to tell you, you have to leave the premises. You have to get out or you will be removed."

Valla and Brandie were stunned. They did not know what he was talking about. They were fearful that they were being notified that James had paid the ultimate sacrifice in Iraq. Again they asked the deputy if James was okay?

He responded that he didn't know, and it was irrelevant to why he was there. He was there to tell them that they needed to immediately leave the premises. Valla and Brandie just looked at each other. While the ultimate sacrifice of war seemed to be diverted at the moment, they were at a loss as to what was happening. The officer knew nothing about James. On one hand, they were immediately overcome with a sense of counting their blessings and great gratitude to their Lord. The officer was not there to give them the worst news possible when a loved one is at war.

On the other hand, life in this world was a continued nightmare with the bank and their attorneys. The deputy informed Valla that according to the paperwork that he received from the court, they were suppose to have left the property a week ago. The deputy said that the bank obtained a default judgment against them because no one went to court. The deputy informed Valla that the court date that the family supposedly missed, was the same date that she had gone to the South Haven Courthouse and met with Attorney Blalock.

How could this happen? Where would they go? Valla, Brandie, and the two girls had to find shelter elsewhere. Valla still believed that she would hear from the court and have an opportunity to set this mess straight. In the meantime, they had to get out. The sheriff deputy told them that he would be back in two days with a crew to remove them.

Valla mentioned a family cabin to Brandie. She had never heard about the family cottage or the family tragedy that prevented James from even visiting the place. However, with just two days to act, Valla felt that they had no choice. All of the furniture in the cabin had been removed years ago, as it had been blood stained during the murders of her nephew and his two friends years earlier. Valla and Brandie's plan was to clear out the house. They had to move beds, a couch, and the kitchen table. Everything else they would move to the barn across the driveway by the Chevy's storage building. Dressers, cabinets, James' clothing, bedroom sets, and pretty much all of James' personal belongings, would be stored away in the barn. Just the bare essentials would go to the cottage. Valla felt she could fix all of this given the fact that she in fact had gone to court the day the deputy said no one was present. The bank's attorney said the hearing was going to be rescheduled.

***

Brandie and Valla were exhausted. They moved everything out of the house. Most of it stayed on the property filling James' workshop, and in the truck bed of his 62' Chevy. The rest went into the storage barn. Only a few truckloads of things went to the cottage, a one-room building that sat among a number of cottages on a lake about five miles away in Bangor, Michigan. Most of them were summer cottages owned by people from Chicago.

With the house empty and the belief they would be back soon, Valla and Brandie steam-cleaned the carpeting and drapes, and cleaned out the fireplace. Always practical, it was an opportune time to do a massive cleaning. While they were exhausted now, upon their return the cleaning would surely be appreciated.

The cabin only had one room for Brandie and the girls. Valla would stay in the old one-car garage that was once was a little storage shed. The shed had open stud-exposed walls and a dirty, concrete floor. There were open rafters and a service door on one end, and a sliding door on the gable end. There were no windows. Buck was left with

James' brother, Steven.

Brandie slept on a couch and the girls had their same beds from home. The cabin had electricity, water, and indoor plumbing. The septic was questionable, and the toilet flow was slow and uncertain. The routine practice for Brandie came to be to only flush the toilet once in the evening—regardless of its accumulation through the day.

Valla slept on an old canvas army cot. She used a plastic five-gallon bucket as a commode during the night and each morning. The shed had electricity and a light switch with a single bulb. During the fall, winter, and early spring months, she could see her breath in the chilly air. Sometimes, in below freezing temperatures, Valla would lie beneath her cocoon of blankets and unzipped sleeping bags and just stare up into the rafters. The pitter-patter of mice and bats were ever so prevalent. At least the high bat population would help with the insects in the warmer months.

She was a strong woman and had not cried much in her life. But, this drove her to tears more nights than not. She was simply frustrated and helpless, knowing they were in the right, and things had gone so wrong. Yet she still had many blessings. James was okay, and he would be able to fix all of this when he came home.

***

Hurley was beside himself thinking of his mother, wife, and their two young children being displaced from his home. His family and his dream home were far beyond his reach. All he could do was try to stay out of harm's way and focus on his war duties. He felt, he would deal with this when he comes home; there was nothing he can do while in Iraq. The JAG officers assured him that everything would be just fine. They explained that the SCRA protects active duty personnel such as himself, from creditors.

The officer understood that to a soldier in a war zone, a foreclosure back home was not only a family crisis, but a major distraction in what was already a precarious and potentially deadly situation. That was exactly why the SCRA does not allow the non-judicial foreclosure and eviction events to take place.

To Hurley, this all sounded really good, however, he was now unable to sleep. What was going on with his family back home was all-consuming. All he did was work and worry about his mother, wife, and two young children who were now living in deplorable conditions. All of the supplies and safety nets that he had set up for them back home were gone. The freezer had been stocked with meat and the apples were in the cellar. Not only was he worried about how his family was going to eat, but also how they were going to find shelter given the conditions of the cottage.

All he did was work and worry about his family. Everyone saw him as a walking zombie. His superior officers had those around him keep a special watch over him. Soldiers in war zones are known to "lose it" over the smallest of issues. Hurley had the Bloody Triangle around him, and a foreign bank stealing his home. Commanding officers in a war zone know that many times the suicide rate among its soldiers can be higher than actual combat casualties. Hurley's situation was deplorable and unbearable for any person to endure. His commanding officers put him on a suicide watch.

CHAPTER 9
FORGING FORWARD

Hurley accepted the JAG officer's advice and forged forward with the helplessness of the situation. A JAG officer is a member of the Judge Advocate General's Corps, which is part of a global network of attorneys within the U.S. Military. They told Hurley the same thing that Valla and Brandie were hearing from the family advocates with the Guard from Fort Custer and Michigan's Capitol in Lansing, Michigan.

James dealt with the odyssey by focusing on his duties in Iraq. He pushed himself twenty hours a day. The stress of keeping the juice flowing and the inherit dangers of electricity were severely taxing, both mentally and physically. The straps of his duffle bag/tool pouch and shoulder bags for his backpack were wreaking havoc on his shoulders and neck. It seemed that he was causing harm to his body every day. He was no longer a kid in his twenties. He always felt fit and kept in great shape, especially for a man in his forties. However, the daily tearing of his neck and shoulders was taking its toll.

His comrades noticed a drastic change in their friend's behavior. He was no longer a chatterbox. No longer did they hear about his fishing and hunting adventures. Wolf Mountain and the Serengetti stories were a thing of the past. Hurley could not talk about Brandie and the girls without choking up at the thought of them being kicked out of his sanctuary. He felt that he had safely set his family up while he was gone.

The moments that he once laid in bed and mentally escaped the war zone with thoughts of home, were now stolen away by a bank and their attorneys. If those folks were with him in Iraq, things would surely be different. But dealing with them would have to wait. His majestic woods were out of his reach and potentially gone. The worry made his stomach sick. Stresses of war, the death, the destruction, or the chances of dying in combat, did not cause the kind of ache and pain that his core now felt. Neither his mother, wife, children, or his home were safe. And there was nothing he could do for them. His role as their protector was pulverized by some foreign bank, which violated United States laws. All while, he was off serving his president, the United States Government and its people. It was maddening pressure and stress unlike any he had ever dealt with before. He was beyond his breaking point.

December 2005 was quickly approaching. Hurley's tour would soon be up. He looked forward to going home and being with his family. He felt an urgency to get his family back in their home. He could not imagine how his mother was enduring the cold of December—let alone how she had gotten through October and November—in that little shed. His homecoming would be their homecoming.

This Christmas he was going to get the biggest Christmas tree ever. This year, the tree was going to cover the entire picture window. The tree would be so tall, that the angel on top would have her head pressed against the ceiling. The tree would stay up until Easter. He was coming home and they were all going to move back to his home set deep in the majestic paradise that he had nurtured for so many years. His homecoming would be everyone's homecoming. He just knew that they were all going back to the river.

During his stay in Iraq, Hurley became an expert power generator mechanic. His training in California really paid off. The advice that he received from returning Vets about supplementing the army-issued tools was spot on. He was able to excel at keeping the juice flowing due to his ability to fabricate tools of his own design. As a welder, he seemed more like an inventor. His toolbox was replete with self-designed and built tools that he had developed through his own war experiences.

The pride and joy of the accomplishments and successes he had in Iraq were only outweighed by the excitement he had for going home. Traveling out of Iraq, and going back home, were only tempered by the physical pain in his neck and right shoulder, and the mental anxiety of getting his home back. Hurley had a great sense of pride for what he was able to accomplish in Iraq. The generators that he was responsible for always flowed power. Hurley's ability to keep the juices flowing kept complete hospitals up and running. Injured and sick troops were able to get the uninterrupted treatment they needed thanks to him.

Command centers kept a consistent flow of planning and implementation of operations...thanks to Hurley juice. He was taking from Iraq, a great sense of pride and accomplishment, and the honor in providing service to his country. He wanted to leave something of himself and help his successors, so he passed on his entire toolbox. All of the tools he personally purchased, and all of the special gadgets and specialty tools that he himself designed and fabricated, were left for the next troop. In a sense, Hurley felt that he could continue to help with the flowing of juice, even while he was gone. He had found his fabricated tools to be invaluable and he could continue to contribute in his own small way to the war effort by passing them on to his replacement.

CHAPTER 10
HOMECOMING

Laura Ingalls Wilder, author of the *Little House* book series once said, "Home is the nicest word there is." Hurley's homecoming was going to be the greatest. He was reuniting with family, and finally ready to get everything back in order. It was clear in his mind that when a soldier comes back from war, he should be able to go back to the home that he had left behind.

Lincoln, and the drafters of the Soldier's and Sailor's Civil Relief Act and the Servicemembers Civil Relief Act, envisioned just what *should have* played out for Hurley's homecoming. A soldier (lucky enough to come home from war) now could deal with his business and family affairs. The creditor's interest rate continued running, and any costs associated with the enforcement of the debt were not forgiven. The creditor loses nothing.

The soldier returns from war and the issues are fairly and truthfully dealt with. James Hurley certainly deserved what had been afforded to U.S. soldiers for more than 150 years. If lenders and creditors are not happy with what the SCRA requires, they are free to go to Congress and seek an amendment of the law. It is not upon predatory lenders to take matters into their own hands and run roughshod over the soldiers.

***

James had never felt such a deep sleep. After twenty-four hours in bed, he asked Brandie how long he had been asleep? He then stayed in bed for two more days. Mentally and physically he was exhausted. His neck and shoulders were killing him. A loud explosion abruptly disturbed his deep rest. James jumped out of bed and dashed across the room to take cover from the incoming RPG attack. The last explosion felt as if it was hitting his unit's quarters. Suddenly, the overwhelming realization of fear and safety combined to really confuse him. He was no longer in Iraq.

While James never wanted to visit, let alone live in the old family cottage, he was enjoying this three-day slumber. He ran outside to determine the cause of the explosion. Of all things, one of his knucklehead neighbors was shooting off a canon. The ridiculousness of someone shooting off a canon on a Saturday morning, among a bunch of lake cottages, reminded James of why he so loved his isolated home set deep in the woods. He always felt that lake homes were always so close together that you could hear the neighbors coughing.

James was ready to end his slumber and go home; to his real home. Brandie naturally brought him back to the cottage where her, Valla, and the girls had been staying for most of the past year. Today, before getting anything to eat, they were going to go home. James was anxious to go check on his property and all of his things. Brandie only brought a few items and some of his clothing to the cottage. They both hurried to get dressed and get the girls together to go home to Hartford—their home on the river.

The drive from Bangor to Hartford only takes a few minutes. Once there, James pulled into his driveway and abruptly stopped just off the road. The house could not be seen from the road. James pleasantly recalled buying the property back in 1994, and being excited about the prospect of a home that could not be seen from the roadway. It had been vacant land with a run-down old shelter. James had envisioned building a home high on the riverbank, set deep in the woods.

Today, he was halted at the head of the driveway that he personally cut through the woods to create. There was a sign that indicated that the property was under surveillance and protected by a security system. He feared being arrested within days of his return from the war. Surely such an occurrence would be ridiculous. This was his home.

James, Brandie, and the girls proceeded up to the home they hadn't been in for more than a year. So many events had taken place; but it seemed like just yesterday that he had left. There were great memories flashing through his head. The girls were in the back seat laughing, yelling, and screaming, "Are we going home, Mommy?"

As they proceeded up the driveway, James noticed his favorite deer stand, and the feelings of the thrill of the upcoming deer season flashed through his mind. The gazebo, the floating dock, and his outbuildings were still there. Everything seemed in its proper place. He was about to get out of the car and go up to his home when Brandie grabbed his forearm and said, "Honey, look at the curtains."

James looked. He really didn't recall what his curtains looked like; he had never closed them before. Part of the great thing about the home's seclusion was that they never had to close the curtains. Now he could see. The curtains were closed. Brandie pulled at his arm and asked to leave. Neither of them were in any condition to confront whoever may be living there. None of it made any sense. Could any of this be possible? What was going on? The Hurleys felt lost and overwhelmed. They were overcome with questions without answers. Was it possible that their home could be lost forever?

Contrary to the attorneys in Iraq, the JAG officers, and their words of encouragement that "they can't do this to you while you are over here," it *was* possible that they could lose their home. James stood there and recalled how he had just driven by a security sign. He was overcome by a sick, sinking feeling. To top it off, Brandie stood next to him and recalled how she and his mother had steam cleaned the carpet and curtains before they left. Valla even cleaned the chimney. Brandie became paralyzed as they both stood there viewing their home.

James had quickly gone from the feelings of exhilaration of a soldier returning home from war, to one of complete sickness. This place was special to him. For ten years, it was his home. Thinking of home was what carried him through the war. He even dreamt of it while in Iraq. His house was the family gathering place for the holidays. The Halloween party where he first met Brandie, was held there. He proposed to and married Brandie right there in the gazebo that he and his brother built one summer. It was the place where his nephews first hunted for squirrels, and where he shot his first big buck.

Everything that defined his existence, and why he volunteered for service in Iraq, was because of this property and the home that he had built. He felt he was living the American dream and he owed it to his country to continue in his military service.

This home made James feel that he had realized that American dream. He served in the Michigan National Guard for twenty-five years. He was proud of his service and the man that he had become. Going to Iraq, and doing what his President told him to do, was the epitome of what he had become and what his country meant to him.

They all returned to the car. James turned to Brandie who was sitting there in complete silence, pale as a ghost. He wondered what had become of his life as he sat in his own driveway, fearing arrest. He was even driving his uncle's car because his vehicle (that Brandie and Valla left at his home) was also gone. Everything that James owned, except for the few personal items that Brandie brought to the cottage, was gone. Everything was lost and neither of them knew what to do.

As they sat in the car, Brandie's immediate attention was drawn to something that would haunt her for the rest of her days. It was something obvious to her, but unseen to him. James was looking at the gazebo where he recalled the morning greetings and sunrise cups of coffee. He once loved to sit there and watch the morning fog roll down the river. He would watch the ducks flow with the current, and the fish surface beneath the sun-glittering waters. This was James' homecoming.

He looked through the window of his shop only to see his Chevy was gone, along with all of his tools. Brandie broke from her shock, and followed James. She was physically ill, and had to vomit when her eyes locked on the sign above James' workshop that he had meticulously carved that read: "Home Sweet Home." The two simply could not comprehend how everything was gone; all of his personal belongings, tools, vehicle, and his 62' Chevy.

It was a very odd experience for both of them. While everything of a personal property nature was gone, everything else was just as they had remembered. The home, stairs they built leading from the deck to the floating dock, the wrap around deck, and the gazebo (everyone's favorite sitting spot). The gazebo sat high above the river and was perfect for seeing sun rises over the river, which flowed for at least 100 yards as it cut up through the woods to the east, to the sunsets as the river flowed past the house to the west, running about another 150 yards. He saw the screened-in porch he built for the hot July summer nights to keep the mosquitos away, the workshop he built especially for his '62 Chevy, the storage barns, the play house, and even his favorite tree stands. Everything was just as he dreamt of it while he tried to sleep in Iraq.

James and Brandie all of the sudden felt scared. The security signs warned of surveillance and what would happen to trespassers. Overcome with aches, frustration, and sickness, they both hurried back into the car. Brandie at first was sobbing uncontrollably and James' eyes welled with tears. As they drove back to the Hurley family cottage, the silence was only broken upon their arrival to the squalid cabin when Brandie asked, "What do we do now?"

He felt he was pushed past his breaking point in Iraq. Now, he simply did not understand the feelings he was experiencing. It seemed that he was on continuous guard duty over his emotions in Iraq; just trying to keep it together. The true reality of the situation had just become known. It was like a brick had hit him square in the face. The sensation of the RPG hitting his tanker in Iraq, shaking the ground, and causing the ringing in his head, was all coming back. He couldn't even answer Brandie. He didn't know what to say. It wasn't going to be all right. He just didn't know.

They returned to the cottage where his cousin and friends were mur-
dered years before. James retreated to the cot in the storage shed. He
couldn't go home. He hated where he was, and the whole world was
spinning. He was sick, and physically and emotionally drained. As
he lay on his mother's cot in the dark and dusty shed, his rage seemed
to blaze.

He could not believe—let alone allow himself—to accept that this was
where his mother was while he was in Iraq…pissing in a bucket. His
mother, wife and children were forced from his home while he was at
war. While he lay on that cot, he watched the dust dance in the cracks
lit by the sunlight, and wondered what had become of his life? He had
returned from war and couldn't go home. Everything he owned before
he left is gone. He didn't even know where his dog was.

James' world was spinning out of control. "This is my homecoming?"
he muttered to himself. "Where is Buck? Buck, Buck, BUCK!" His
old buddy Buck was a magnificent black lab who always seemed to be
smiling. Buck's only mission in life is to please his master. Thinking
of that put James in another panic. After extended training camps,
James would return to Buck, who was pleasantly hysterical in his
greeting. Buck would jump, howl, cry, and drive his head into James'
stomach. That was Buck's way of saying welcome home.

James would always plan their greeting outside to give Buck the room
to jump and squeal, and allow for the too excited droplets and streams
of urine.

"Where is Buck?" Of course Brandie couldn't hear James yelling. He
was in a shed across the yard from the squalid cabin…his family's new
home. James made a solemn oath to avenge those that had done this
to him and his family.

CHAPTER

WHAT NOW?

The following day, after going to town and getting some breakfast, James and his family headed to his uncle Stanley Muvrin's home. Stanley was in his late 70s. He had always been a positive figure in James' life. He spent most of his life working as a realtor; surely he could help figure out what to do. Stanley checked with the Van Buren County Register of Deeds office to see if there had been anything recorded on the property.

In the chain of title, James' interest should be the last recorded deed. Stanley went numb when it was reported by the Van Buren County Registrar that there had been a foreclosure, Sheriff's Deed, and conveyance to a new owner. It was now December of 2005. James had purchased the property in 1994.

Relevant dates of action regarding the Hurley foreclosure:

2004

July 2: The Michigan Department of Military and Veteran Affairs ordered James to active duty at Camp Roberts, California for training from July 21-August 20.

September 9: The U.S. Army ordered James to active duty in support of Operation Iraqi Freedom for an initial period of 18 months, to begin on October 1. *Note: As of this date, James and his family, were protected by the Servicemembers' Civil Relief Act. After a non-judicial foreclosure action, as was done against the Hurley family, there is a six-month redemption period. the bank initiated the non-judicial foreclosure action shortly after James returned from his military training in California.

October 14: The defendants held a Sheriff's Sale. The sale occurred following the notice by publication, which contained the defendants' sworn affidavit stating that:

The undersigned, being first duly sworn, states that upon investigation he is informed that none of the persons named in the notice attached to the sheriff's deed of mortgage foreclosure, nor any person upon whom they or any of them were dependent, were in the military service of the United States as the time of sale or for six months prior thereto; nor the present grantees.

The undersigned further states that this Affidavit is made for purposes of preserving a record and clearing title by virtue of the Soldiers and Sailors Relief Act of 1940, as amended.

Someone subject to foreclosure has six months to pay off the bank's balance and the homeowner can keep their home; they redeem their interest. Under the SCRA, the clock never runs while the soldier is on active duty. The redemption period limitation of six months is extended until the solider is off active duty. The SCRA even allows additional time after the active duty so that the soldier is able to return home, and get their affairs in order before they have to act to protect their interest. The redemption period is tolled; stopped. The period does not commence to run until ninety days *after* the active duty period ends.

Under the SCRA, the non- judicial foreclosure against James and his family was illegal. A non-judicial foreclosure cannot be brought against an active duty soldier. A bank may try and obtain a judicial foreclosure, which would require a judge to determine that James' military service did not have a negative impact on his ability to defend the case. Clearly, if the bank had sought a judicial foreclosure, a judge would have halted the action until James' return from his war service in Iraq.

Contrary to the SCRA, the bank forged forward with its illegal fore-closure, even though by April, 2005 the bank, its attorneys, and the mortgage servicing company were fully aware of James' active duty status. They continued forward with the running of the redemption period, illegal foreclosure, numerous false affidavits, declared the ex-piration of the redemption period (that really didn't exist, let alone run) only to allow and fuel the lies and deception conveyed to the judge in court through the eviction proceedings.

Just two months before James' returned from Iraq, Stanley saw that there was a deed from the bank to some purchaser out of Chicago. Nothing made sense to the Hurleys. Stanley was telling them that James no longer owned his home, and that another family held the title.

James had to do something, but what? Stanley echoed what James had heard so many times from the JAG officers while he was in Iraq, "They cannot do this." *Well,* James thought. *They did, and my home is gone.*

Stanley encouraged James to call a lawyer. His friends in the VFW told him to call a lawyer. The Veterans Affairs Office in Lansing could not help him, so he would have to talk to a civilian lawyer. On the television and in the yellow pages, there are numerous advertisements and listings of attorneys. William Shatner of *Star Trek,* and the famous actor Robert Vaughn, were spokespersons on commercials for some pretty good-sounding lawyers. The yellow pages had full-page ads by lawyers, with some even covering the entire back cover of the book.

After calling four law firms that James saw on television, three dif-ferent firms that were featured on phone book covers, and two from yellow page ads (which all promised "a personal touch for your case – no case too big or small"), James was ready to give up. He could not find help. He spent over seven months, most of 2006, meeting and talking with lawyers. Sometimes he felt like he had a sympathetic ear, but they all ended their review of his claim with disappointment. Sometimes he would waste weeks, and even months with a few of the lawyers only to learn they were not interested.

Phone book covers and yellow page ads did not help. Some of the more personal, smaller ads would give him lawyers who gave him a more caring turn down. James spent seven months going through a dozen offices from Grand Rapids to Kalamazoo, St. Joseph to Benton Harbor, and every county in between. He sought the mega/multi-city large firms, mid-sized small firms, and even solo practitioners. No one was interested. Even legal liaison officers for Veterans didn't know what to do, and would just refer the Hurleys to another lawyer that couldn't help. Stanley would not let James give up. This wasn't right. Stanley told him that he needed a lawyer that had been around for a while, and had a sense of right and wrong…and a willingness to help people.

The county seat for Van Buren County is in the Village of Paw Paw. It is a small rural town of a few thousand people set in Southwest Michigan. It is mostly a bedroom community for Kalamazoo, a city of about a quarter million people and home to Western Michigan University, Kalamazoo Valley Community College, and Kalamazoo College. Van Buren County has a beautiful lakeshore along Lake Michigan. Much of the county has a sandy soil and coupled with the airflow from the Great Lakes, is highly conducive to fruit growth. Welch's and Coca-Cola have plants in the county in order to be in close proximity to the fruit production for their juices and other products.

For more than twenty years, Matthew R. Cooper practiced law and helped people throughout Van Buren County and Southwest Michigan. Stanley recalled Matt from his involvement with community Optimist Clubs. Matt had been the president of the Paw Paw Optimist Club for more than six years, and was committed to keeping the club alive in Paw Paw. It had once been the largest service club in town. With most of its members having passed away, Matt was trying to keep the club in existence for one of the club's charter members. Stanley admired Matt's commitment and thought he surely would be the kind of person that could provide James with some good advice.

James found the listing for Matt in the Paw Paw phone book, just a single line listing with a phone number—no ad. Stanley called and got

Peggy, Matt's longtime receptionist. After a pleasant conversation and a brief synopsis, Peggy made James an appointment. For a small-town general practice law office, the firm actually had a presence throughout the State of Michigan. Matt had represented a multitude of clients, including major litigation cases, which resulted in jury trials in Van Buren, Kalamazoo, Barry, and Wayne Counties, and had appeared in over seventeen Michigan counties. Matt had also prosecuted cases in Illinois, Maryland, Indiana, as well as Michigan at the Federal and State Court levels.

He had handled cases in the Western and Eastern Federal District Courts, the United States 6th Circuit Court of Appeals, the Michigan Court of Appeals, and the Michigan Supreme Court. He had been selected as the Chamber of Commerce Community Volunteer of the Year, and sat on numerous county-wide boards, including various statewide committees with the State Bar Association.

Stanley accompanied James and Brandie, who went with much skepticism and a forlorn attitude. So many other big firms and prestigious lawyers had passed on the case. Either the lawyer was looking for the easy case, for easy money, or they just honestly were afraid of dealing with a Servicemembers' Civil Relief Act case. Some of the attorneys would admittedly acknowledge that it was a very obscure area of the law that they had never dealt with before, and would feel just too uncomfortable trying to be involved with such a foreign area of the law.

The Hurleys felt that they needed to find someone who was truly interested in helping people, and who would not be afraid to deal with something so unusual.

CHAPTER

FINALLY

J ames and Brandie first met Matt Cooper in the fall of 2006. It had been two years since the illegal foreclosure forced his family to live in the old family cabin. For James, it had been a year since his return from fighting in Iraq; and had been fighting for his home ever since.

There seemed to be an immediate mutual connection between Matt and the Hurleys. Unfortunately, Matt had never dealt with the Servicemembers Civil Relief Act. During their first meeting, Matt had some kind of recollection of the Soldiers' and Sailors' Civil Relief Act.

He had a general familiarity with the Act that protects soldiers from creditors while serving on active duty. He knew that, before any type of lawsuit against anyone was filed—whether an auto-accident, dog bite case, or divorce proceeding—a preamble must be filed to declare if the defendant is in the military. Knowing this, Matt immediately believed that something was not right. Given the travesty of the circumstances, he felt compelled to dig deeper.

Typically, fairness has no place in the courtroom or our justice system. However, Matt had always practiced from a perspective that there is a right and wrong. And, he felt the justice system has an underlying premise to seek the truth to determine right from wrong. Clearly, a U.S. Soldier should not go off to war for his country and come back to find someone else living in his home. The basic premise of the pre-suit declaration about military service caused Matt to have the strong feeling that somehow James was protected from foreclosure and eviction.

Finally, James and Brandie truly felt that it was their lucky day after they met Matt and saw his determination toward the truth. Not only was Matt willing to look into their case, he was not asking for any money up front. Matt's initial hurdle in his research of the SCRA came when he learned that it was no longer referred to as the Soldiers' and Sailors' Civil Relief Act.

In 1940, before the United States entered into World War II, Congress reenacted the Soldiers' and Sailors' Civil Relief to "expedite the national defense under the emergent conditions which are threatening the peace and security of the United States..." In substance, the 1940 Act is identical with the 1918 Act that Congress mulled over throughout 1917 with the looming of World War I. In 1917, it was clear that Congress intended an Act, for "protection against suit to men in military service", as various State statutes had supported during the Civil War. After congressional action in 1917, the 1918 Act was the first national Soldier's Relief Act.

Matt proceeded with the firm belief that the Hurleys had a claim under the Act. He felt that the bank, its lawyers who signed a false affidavit, and the mortgage servicing company violated §533 and §526 of the Servicemembers Civil Relief Act. Under §526, "a period of military service may not be included in the computing of the period provided for the redemption". Therefore, the sale of the Hurley property in April, 2005 was illegal.

Matt took the position that the illegal possession and wrongful sale were commenced with the use of a false affidavit. To him, that amounted to theft by the bank, which was perpetrated by the attorneys and mortgage servicing company as its agents. In legal terms, that type of theft is defined under the Michigan Conversion Act, which concerns personal property.

According to the SCRA, the Hurleys were entitled to actual damages, as well as punitive damages (extraordinary damages permitted in rare circumstances to allow for the punishment of a wrongdoer). Neither Matt—nor any other attorney he knew—ever obtained punitive damages. Under Michigan law, the availability of punitive damages was a thing of the past. Matt was hopeful that under this Act, that he was reading for the first time, it may present a situation where he might have a crack at punitive damages.

***

Matt grew up in Portage, Michigan, a small town in Kalamazoo County. He graduated cum laude, from Western Michigan University in 1986. After he completed Valparaiso University School of Law in 1989, he fulfilled a one-year clerkship for the Honorable Phillip D. Schaefer, Circuit Court Judge for the County of Kalamazoo. The following year, he began practicing in Paw Paw (just outside Kalamazoo) with Harold Schuitmaker, and later was joined by Theresa Cypher and Brian Knotek.

Matt and his wife, Laurie, settled on a small farm in Paw Paw's fruit belt. The beautiful piece of property allowed Matt, Laurie and their three children (Anella, Drew, and Bennett) to enjoy living a life among the wilderness, much like the Hurleys. Paw Paw is known for its sandy soil and climate, which is conducive for growing concord grapes, tart cherries, and Muvrin apples. The Cooper family spent countless hours hiking the surrounding farmland. The family had fun hunts for morel mushrooms. They also found seashell fossils, ancient sea coral and Petoskey stones that were left from the glaciers that cut through the area as the Great Lakes were formed thousands of years ago.

Matt's practice consisted mostly of general civil litigation, auto accidents, premises liability, estate planning, probate administration, real estate, and some criminal cases. His love for his community led to him incorporating and obtaining charitable organization status for the Paw Paw Rocket Football, Cheer, and Youth Baseball programs. He was heavily involved with the Paw Paw Area Rotary Club, and served as the Paw Paw Optimist Club president for numerous years. His ability to wear many different hats gave him the ability and confidence to take up, and move forward with the Hurley case.

Matt's first strategy (something he did in various cases) was to determine if there is a way to resolve a case peacefully, without a lawsuit. A lawsuit can be an all-out war, and before the gauntlet is thrown and fighting commences, an amicable resolution is always advisable. Common belief among many plaintiff lawyers is that the best time to settle a case with a defendant (or a defendant and their insurance company) is before suit is filed. This would most likely be before the potential defendants have outside counsel involved. In-house counsel is typically paid a salary, where outside counsel charges private, hourly billing.

Insurance companies have professional, mostly in-house adjusters, and businesses such as hospitals and banks have their own risk loss management departments that welcome the opportunity to adjust a claim before the commencement of a lawsuit. Once defense attorneys get involved and their meters start running, a case will not be resolved until it has been sufficiently "milked" by the defense attorney. Defense attorneys are not necessarily begrudged, it is merely a fact of how the process works; in fairness to them, they cannot fairly try and resolve a case without sufficient discovery and time to ascertain the merits, weaknesses, and strengths of a case.

Christmas time 2006, led to many sleepless nights for Matt. He worried over the Hurley case. With 2007 approaching, it had been well over two years since the foreclosure. Some Statutes of Limitations of cases involve six-month periods, one-year periods, two-years, or even six-year periods of limitation. Matt had no idea what time periods were involved with an SCRA case. The Statute of Limitations issue, and the SCRA was not clear; it added an element of anxiety. Missing the Statute of Limitations on a case is something feared by any attorney concerned about malpractice.

Nevertheless, Matt chose to make contact and negotiate a resolution with the defendants in hopes to get James' property back. The goal to reclaim the property was unrealistic. Matt's fear was that the Hurley home and property was out of reach, because the property had been sold to a bona fide purchaser. All he could do was hope the defendants could work with the Hurleys, and the new buyer to agree to sell the property back to James. His attempt to contact the new owners was ignored. He didn't want to push the new owner too hard and he felt the best go between would be the bank, servicing agent, and the attorneys that conveyed the property to the new owners.

Christmas 2006 went by without hearing anything from any of the potential three defendants. Matt's attempts to contact the bank, mortgage servicing company and attorneys fell on deaf ears. Since returning in December 2005, the Hurleys had been living in the cottage. The first thing James did, after he learned that they would not be going home, was to make room for Valla to move in from the shed. Shortly thereafter, he updated the water well and septic so that both were in good working order.

James was committed to constructing a large addition for living quarters that would attach to the main portion of the cottage. Even though the foreclosure was illegal, it still destroyed James' credit. His construction projects were strictly confined to only purchase building materials with cash. He lived paycheck to paycheck, which greatly reduced the extra cash available for construction materials. He built a large shell around the entire cottage that, over time he could complete in different sections. He felt an immediate need to get new quarters for Valla, and something for him and Brandie outside of the main cottage area. He was still haunted by the murder of his cousin and the friends that happened there, but he made do the best he could under the circumstances.

Mid-January 2007 found everyone patiently waiting for some type of response from the defendants. Given what the Hurleys had gone through, they had nothing but patience and a sense of comfort knowing that they had an attorney who was trying to do something for them. They felt a bond and a trust for Matt, who was about the same age as James. Matt was friendly, open, patient, and willing to listen to their concerns and questions. They truly felt that they had found the type of attorney that their Uncle Stanley said they would need—someone who really cared and truly has a desire to help people.

After weeks of waiting in vain, Matt resent letters to the bank's attorneys and its mortgage servicing company. The first round of letters went out by regular mail. The second round was sent by regular and certified mail, which required a return receipt. After it was clear that the defendants received written notification, all three received numerous phone calls, and more letters, to no avail. All roads, and any contact seemed to point toward a potential contact with a representative of the mortgage servicing company in Texas.

In seventeen years of practice, Matt had never been put off, or faced such a wall of delay as much as he had by the mortgage-servicing representative in Texas. It was less frustrating and annoying to just be ignored than to deal with an individual that would never have any straight answers or direction to try and resolve a situation and dispute. The representatives in Texas were simply trying to delay and frustrate Matt, as they had absolutely no interest to resolve the claims.

Before filing suit, Matt needed to have some understanding of the SCRA and how such a case would proceed. In addition, he spent months in attempts to have some meaningful discussions with anyone involved in the foreclosure, however, it had become a complete waste of time.

HOW DO YOU FILE A
SCRA LAWSUIT?

In May 2007, Matt filed suit in a court 200 miles east of Paw Paw, in Federal District Court in Detroit, Michigan. He would represent both James and Brandie. Before filing suit, he could not find anyone that could explain to him how to file an SCRA case. Matt called guard representatives in Lansing and Washington, D.C. Many could tell Matt how to defend against a claim utilizing the SCRA protections as a shield, but no one could explain how to use it as a sword.

Matt found a senior retired officer that led him to a guy, who led him to a guy, who led him to another guy, who led him to an attorney in Maryland, who told him to call this lawyer in Shreveport, Louisiana. Colonel John S. Odom, Jr., was suppose to be a real nice guy, and was someone who really knew his stuff about the SCRA. When he worked in the Pentagon, he helped draft the Amendments of 2003. Almost every day, he received a call from someone in the United States (from Federal or State judges to practicing attorneys or professors or soldiers), in trouble regarding SCRA. He helped them all. Matt gave him a call.

Colonel Odom does not recall the details of the first time he spoke over the phone with Matt about the Hurley case. However, it was in May of 2007 that, after their conversation, Matt had the confidence to jump head first into the dark abyss of the Hurley case. The colonel's willingness to share his wisdom and knowledge about the SCRA was invaluable.

Matt had begun the case on his own, but he knew his priority was to get assistance. He established a nice connection with Col. Odom and felt that the colonel would be willing to provide assistance in the future. In addition, there was an immediate concern about having independent counsel for Brandie. The SCRA (as Matt understood it) seemed to provide a separate and independent cause of action for her, as James' dependent. Under the SCRA, a soldier's dependent could have her own independent cause of action and not merely a derivative-type claim.

Over the years, Matt established a friendship and sound professional relationship with one of this country's best litigators, Attorney Frank B. Melchiore of St. Petersburg, Florida. Shortly after commencement of the suit, Matt attempted to recruit him to file an Appearance on behalf of Brandie. Matt was also smart enough, and unselfish enough to know that in a case of this magnitude, complexity, and importance, he needed as much help as possible. Matt had filed suit against one of the world's largest banks, one of the United States' largest mortgage servicing companies, and one of the largest foreclosure law firms in the Midwest. He would have to face a team of numerous attorneys on behalf of each defendant.

Melchiore's experience as a litigator led him to handle some of the most complex auto, products, and professional malpractice type cases. However, neither Melchiore nor Col. Odom were involved directly in the court action. Matt had discussions with them, but no one was on board or had an appreciation for the shit storm that was about to come. Melchiore's earliest memory of talking about the case before his involvement—and perhaps one of the reasons for his hesitation to get involved—was that clearly, the case would not be resolved without a trial.

This was completely new terrain for everyone involved. Melchiore's consistent warning to Matt, whenever the two discussed the Hurley case, was that this case would have to be tried. Since filing suit, the once quiet and non-existent attitude taken by the potential defendants (now that they were real defendants in a Federal District Court lawsuit), had woken the sleeping bear. The defendant bank, one of our world's largest, was being sued by attorney Matt Cooper of Paw Paw, Michigan; the president of the Paw Paw Area Rotary Club and Paw Paw Rocket Football assistant coach.

The battle lines had been drawn. They had either ignored or pushed aside the Hurleys' claims, so they were sued. The defendants filed simple answers to the Hurley Complaint.

The law firm that was sued answered on May 23, 2007. The mortgage servicing company and the bank's answers were filed on June 1, 2007. The court's scheduling order, which lay out how the case would proceed, set the Hurley Trial for August 8, 2008. After filing the initial answers, the defendants felt it was preposterous that little ole James Hurley and Matt Cooper from Paw Paw, would dare bring a Federal lawsuit against them. In October 2007, the defendants counter-sued Sgt. James Hurley seeking in excess of $50,000. A week later, the defendants filed offers of judgement with the court of $3,000 by the law firm, and $1,000 by the bank.

An Offer of Judgment is a means set up by the court through court rules for the parties to settle the case. It is an aggressive tactic to make an offer of judgment. The defendants offered the Hurleys $4,000 to settle the case. By court rule, if the Hurleys rejected the offer and did not do better at trial, they could be assessed the costs and fees incurred by the defendants. Essentially, the defendants were threatening the Hurleys to possibly have to pay the defendants hundreds of thousands of dollars. It was their way of telling the Hurleys that they should just go away. Matt was hoping to help the Hurleys, not cause them more pain and suffering…the exact feeling the defendants hoped to instill in the Hurleys and their attorney.

The Federal Court system for the Eastern and Western Districts of Michigan is paperless. Through a registration system with the courts, attorneys admitted to practice in Federal Court can file pleadings with the court through the Internet. Each pleading is added to the docket sheet for a particular case in sequential, numerical order as it is filed.

An appearance with a complaint starts a cause of action and is typically first on the docket sheet. Sometimes a case is resolved within five to ten docket entries.

On average throughout Federal Courts, cases are resolved within eight months and have a limited number of docket entries ranging from twenty to seventy. The Federal filing system known as the PACER (Public Access to Court Electronic Records) System is an electronic public access and docket information from Federal Appellate, District, and Bankruptcy courts.

The Hurley case, filed in May 2007, would not be heard until March of 2011, and had approximately 385 docket entries. It would be the first time in the history of the United States that a jury was seated to hear a SCRA case. In December 2007, all of the defendants joined together in a Motion to Dismiss. The defendants wanted the judge to just throw the whole case out. Aside from their theory that there was no such thing as a SCRA case, these defendants felt that they actually did the Hurleys a favor by getting them out from underneath the property and debt they just could not afford—or so the argument went. The defendants' first response to the Hurleys' pre-suit claim was met with contempt by some of the potential defendants, and simply ignored by the others. It left Matt no choice but to file a lawsuit. In open court, on their first motion to request the court to dismiss the case, the defense attorneys were hostile, disrespectful, and arrogant.

Judge Edmunds, the judge in the Eastern District, met their incredulous behavior head on by denying their motion. She scolded the defendants by declaring on the record, "clearly the defendants have really screwed up here and they need to make it right and make it right fast."

Make it right fast, the judge told them. The case would drag on for more than four more years. Historical events would unfold. The defendants obviously did not like Edmunds ruling, or her apparent feelings about the case. They asked the court to dismiss the case, and argued that the SCRA does not provide for a private cause of action. And, that a soldier who has sustained a loss or has suffered because someone has violated the very rights protected by the SCRA, cannot bring a lawsuit based on those violations. They claimed that the SCRA could only be used as a shield by the soldier, to seek the protections afforded when he defends a claim.

Such a position by the defense was simply astonishing. How can a soldier away at war assert a defense in a lawsuit when he or she is at war and unable to defend him or herself? Or, especially in this case, where the foreclosure was nonjudicial?

Further, previous court rulings set the precedent that the SCRA does indeed provide for a private cause of action. Aside from the damages provisions contained in the Act itself (which would not exist other than allowing for it to be in a cause of action) all of the previous rulings followed the simple premise that Congress would not provide rights without allowing for a remedy from their violation. Where there is no remedy, what good is a right? The Hurley case is exactly what Congress envisioned. If a soldier's rights under the SCRA are violated when he is taking up arms for his country, the soldier can certainly avail himself of his country's court system to protect those rights.

Cooper and Hurley decided to file the case in Detroit because that was the most proper venue. All of the defendants do business there, and one of the defendants was located there. There is also no denying the fact that plaintiffs in general prefer the Eastern part of Michigan as opposed to the ultra conservative folks in the Western District of Michigan. There is also a preference of the Eastern District over the Western District, given that one of the most conservative cities in Michigan is in the Western District, Grand Rapids; also a major banking center in the Midwest. Considering Judge Edmunds' decision and denial of the defendants' Motion to Dismiss, the defendants certainly did not want her on the case, and filed a Motion for Change of Venue.

The case was pending for ten months before the motion was filed. Surprisingly, Judge Edmunds granted the Motion and the case was moved to the Western District, and assigned to Judge Maloney in Kalamazoo. Hurley and Cooper, while disappointed, lived their lives knowing that it was always better to count your blessings than to allow negatives to draw you down. At least the case wasn't going to Grand Rapids, and Judge Maloney was a fair judge that could be trusted. In addition, Kalamazoo was much closer, and would be a lot more practical than either Detroit or Grand Rapids if the case was going to require a lot of hearings in court. The Detroit Courthouse was almost three hours away, and Grand Rapids was about half of that. Kalamazoo's Courthouse was simply thirty minutes away from Cooper's law office.

The defendant had distance against them, but, the case moved to a much more conservative area. Matt reassured James that this was not a setback. While they loved Edmunds' initial reaction to the case, they had faith that Maloney would do great—at least it wasn't in Grand Rapids. The wheels of justice move slowly. Typically, a civil case progresses through the system in approximately eighteen to twenty-four months. If there are appeals involved, it can take up to three years.

Matt felt the Hurley case would move quickly given the clear SCRA violations and Judge Edmunds' comments on their behalf. Judge Edmunds scheduled the matter for trial within that year. Maloney was known as a tough workhorse. He too would keep it moving.

INTO THE SYSTEM

T he case commenced in May of 2007. It was the hope that by Christmas of that year, the light at the end of the tunnel would be seen. Unfortunately, that December saw the counter claim, offer of judgment, and the Motion to Dismiss. Not even two months after the case was transferred to Kalamazoo, Judge Maloney recused himself. Approximately thirteen months after the case was initiated, the case was reassigned to an ultra-conservative judge. The President George H. W. Bush appointee, Judge Gordon J. Quist would have control of the case…in Grand Rapids!

In addition, it was a busy time for Matt, his wife Laurie, and their children. Anella, the oldest, was involved with tennis and the high school band. Matt was the coach for Drew and Bennett's baseball and football teams, and was treasurer of Paw Paw Rocket Football. The Paw Paw Youth Rocket Football program may be one of the most unique in the country. Matt's work was exemplified through the generosity of NFL All-Pro Jason Babin whose career began when he was a child participant in Paw Paw Rocket Football.

In 2000, Matt became the treasurer of Paw Paw Rocket Football, Inc. When the previous treasurer turned over a shoebox with various receipts and documents contained inside, the program was in the red. Thanks to a very active mother in the community, Terri Williams, the program was turned around. And through the involvement of Matt and Jason Babin, it became a role model for other programs.

Paw Paw is a small community and does not have a youth football program that is connected to the school system, local government, nor any type of parks and recreation program. It is an entity unto itself. In 2004, Jason Babin was selected in the first round of the NFL draft. He is an All-Pro player that would go on to play more than thirteen seasons in the NFL. Matt was friends with Jason's mother and father, Tina and Jim. Together, they asked if Jason would be able to make some type of contribution to the Paw Paw Rocket Football program?

Jim, a former Paw Paw Rocket Football standout in his own right, said that if the following conditions were met, Jason would consider donating: (1) that Paw Paw Rocket Football become a legal entity; (2) that Paw Paw Rocket Football have a long-term lease agreement with automatic renewal provisions with the Village of Paw Paw for a football field; and (3) that the program obtain a non-profit tax-exempt status.

Matt incorporated Paw Paw Rocket Football, Inc., under the laws of the State of Michigan and went to work obtaining Recognition as a tax-exempt organization under Section 501(c)(3) of the Internal Revenue Code. Immediately upon hearing of these accomplishments, Jason gave, and continues to give generously to the football program. Not only has he contributed out of his own pocket, but he has also worked with the National Football League to obtain matching funds.

Jason further encouraged, and worked with Under Armor to provide direct donations to the program. At one time, Paw Paw Rocket Football, Inc., handed equipment out to the children through used grocery bags. Because of the generosity of Jason and Under Armor, there are years where the children received their equipment and new shoes in Under Armor duffle bags. Not only did the 501(c)(3) status allow the generous donations through Jason Babin, the NFL, and Under Armor, but the generosity of some caused a contagious effect among all of the participants in the program.

For example, one of the coaches, through his company, worked to build a new stadium for Kalamazoo College. Quickly he saw the value of getting Kalamazoo College to donate the old score boards to the

Paw Paw Program. Matt also obtained 501(c)(3) status for Paw Paw Youth Baseball, Inc. The programs obtained new (Kalamazoo College's old) score boards for their fields.

In addition, many companies such as State Farm and Pfizer donated. Thanks to the generosity of Jason Babin, and the efforts put forth by Matt, Paw Paw Rocket Football, Inc., has youth programs that provide services to around 200 kids each year, and is actually able to receive donations from the NFL.

Through it all, Matt had a full case load. He was busy with cases from criminal to one of a little old lady who was sued by the Village of Paw Paw because of chipped paint in her hallway, and other code violations. While in the middle of the Hurley case, he was constantly interrupted by phone calls that led to pro bono work. Frequently, Matt would be in the middle of working on a Hurley pleading, only to get interrupted by a 45-minute phone call with zero billing opportunity.

Matt realized that so much work in a community like Paw Paw is pro bono. His life was hectic and he seemed to fly by the seat of his pants. He couldn't have even begun to do any of what he did without his wonderful wife Laurie. She was the caretaker, an educated nurse, a dedicated stay-at-home mom, and even worked as a hospice nurse on the weekends.

In the meantime, James and Brandie were trying to rebuild their lives. Most of James' personal possessions were gone. The bank and new owner dumped and hauled away everything that Valla and Brandie so carefully stored away in the barns and sheds. James' 62' Chevy was gone. Even their dog was gone. The tiny cottage and congested lake neighborhood was no place for Buck.

James still served in the guard, and as a veteran of Iraq he was able to secure a good paying civilian job at Fort Custer in Battle Creek. With a good job and money coming in, he started to make the Hurley cottage (a place that he never wanted to visit again) into a place that his family could comfortably live. The one-room cottage was transformed and no longer resembled what it once was.

With his credit totally destroyed by the illegal foreclosure, James could not get any type of financing for a vehicle, let alone building supplies. He bought an old truck on credit from his Uncle Stanley. He bought lumber every week to build as they could afford to pay with cash. While there had not been any productive settlement talks before suit, once it had been filed, it was hopeful that the defense would now have some interest in an amicable resolution. However, as the case stayed in Grand Rapids, there had yet to be any settlement discussions.

It was still the bank's position that they did the Hurleys a favor. The defense rejoiced with Edmunds' departure, the assignment of Quist, and the case now being in Grand Rapids. The bank that violated James' SCRA rights filed their counter pleadings and sued James and Brandie for the deficiency the bank sustained when they sold his property. At the time of illegal foreclosure, James owed approximately $100,391.71 on the mortgage. The bank sold James' property for approximately $76,000.00. Therefore, the bank was now suing James *and* Brandie for the deficiency of $51,642.01 even though Brandie was not even a party on the mortgage!

There was no better place than a city known as a major banking center of the Midwest, to have a bank sue an individual for a deficiency balance. Now, James and Brandie were faced with the possibility of having to pay the bank that illegally stole and sold their home.

Photos Gallery

THE WAR FRONT

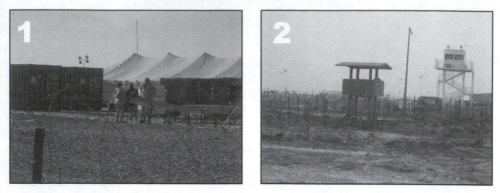

1) Sgt. James Hurley took photos during his stay in Kuwait such as this one of the tents the soldiers called home during their deployment.
2) The watch towers along the perimeter at TQ.

3) The convoy prepares to leave Kuwait.
4) This bunker was three times larger than Sgt. Hurley's bunker.

5) A bunker is located behind the semi-truck trailers and Comex trailers, which had been converted into living quarters.
6) Soldiers drive down a road in Iraq to the forward operational base. TQ.

7) Sgt. Hurley poses during the caravan.
8) This explosion in the distance was a common occurrence.

9) One of Suddam Hussein's planes found at TQ. It was one of many found
   around TQ that US Troops uncovered and disabled.
10) The platform behind the generator mechanics' shop.

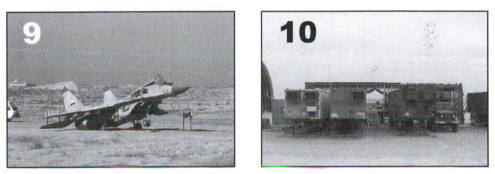

11) These were the living quarters for some mechanics.
12) One of the soldiers takes a $5 camel ride in Kuwait.

THE HOME FRONT

13-15) James returns home to find another owner has purchased it. He is pictured here at the home and outbuildings along the river.

16) James and Brandie were married in this gazebo. Brandie once found peace here each morning.

17) James on a bridge along the roadway in front of his former home. His home is unseen over his shoulder through the woods.

18) The river from the deck of the gazebo.

19) Sgt. Hurley is recognized for his exemplary service.

20) The place James called home before being deployed.

Photos 17, 20 and 21
Erik Holladay - Photographer
Used with permission by the
New York Times.

21) Attorney Matthew R. Cooper and James Hurley during their court battle.

THE DEFENDANTS ARE
ON A ROLL

Judge Edmunds is gone. The Defendants moved the case to Grand Rapids. The case was assigned to Judge Quist. The Defendants now sued the Hurleys for more than $50,000 for a deficiency. On June 6, 2008 and docket entry #100 the defendants filed a Motion for Sanctions against Attorney Matt Cooper. Why not? These defendants had set the country's protections for its soldiers on its head. Make all those that oppose them pay. If they want to make the soldier pay, at the very least they should make his attorney pay as well.

The basis for the Motion for Sanctions against Matt was to claim that he made up sections of the SCRA; claiming the citations he used did not exist. Matt cited Colonel Huckabee who was the drafter of the most recent amendments, and the one who actually renamed the Act. While the Motion for Sanctions was seen as frivolous by the Magistrate, she nevertheless scolded Matt for complicating the case and questioned him why he had some other lawyer filing his Appearance on behalf of Brandie? Matt left the courtroom bewildered. How he could actually be made to feel bad after he had just prevailed in a Motion for Sanctions against him?

The previous Christmas, Matt was alone in the case as he drafted responses to Defendants' Motions to Dismiss. At that time, Matt prevailed in Detroit. The following year in Grand Rapids, the defendants made another attempt to have the case dismissed without a trial by filing Motions for Summary Judgment. Essentially, the defendants made the same arguments that they tried to make in Detroit with their Motions to Dismiss.

Alone, Matt with his legal assistant Lisa, faced dozens of attorneys from mega-sized law firms. The bank's lead counsel hired a mega-firm to assist in the litigation. There would be three to four attorneys at her disposal with a highly experienced and seasoned attorney who lead the litigation battle. Oddly, every twelve to fourteen months, the attorneys in the mega-firm withdrew and another firm and its litigation department hotshots would appear. They all came with their own little bag of tricks and hostilities. The bank's attorney went through three, then four firms until they settled with the firm that would eventually try the case—three months before trial.

At this time, the case stood in a different posture from Matt's per-spective. He had enlisted the assistance of Frank Melchiore and Dan Romano. Shortly after filing in Detroit, Matt brought Dan on board as his office was located in Detroit. While the case was in Detroit, Matt knew the benefits of having an attorney in town. He would need to have someone attend court on a moment's notice, as well as a local office to conduct meetings and conferences associated with the case progression.

Matt was very pleased that Frank agreed to come on board to represent Brandie. For many years, Matt and Frank worked on cases together when Frank lived and practiced law primarily in Michigan. For many years, Frank lived with his wife Sarah in South Haven, Michigan. He worked for a large Plaintiff's litigation firm with Michigan offices in Kalamazoo, Detroit, Grand Rapids, and Traverse City. Aside from his love of Florida, and due to the negative effects and drastic measures that Michigan took relative to tort reform, Frank relocated to St. Petersburg, Florida.

Retired Michigan Supreme Court Chief Justice Elizabeth A. Weaver, has asserted in her book *Judicial Deceit*, that Michigan's high court and the state's judicial system has been, and is corrupt. Through the many contacts that Frank still had in Michigan, he maintained an office there and watched his practice grow to handle cases all over the country.

Frank and his wife Sarah, enjoyed a very busy and active life along the gulf shores of Florida with their Miniature Schnauzer, Sugar. Both Frank and his wife are very career orientated, and yet very focused on their families, in addition to being caregivers to their elderly parents and assisting elderly friends in their community.

Dan and Frank agreed with the nutshell characterizations Matt attached to the case. Obviously, the defendants were bad, and did something really wrong. Matt felt that he had just scratched the surface with the Hurley case. The defendants argued that James was not entitled to SCRA protections because he never sent the bank or mortgage servicing company his individual active duty orders.

The SCRA provides active duty military personnel the opportunity to have a maximum interest rate on their loan obligations of six percent. If a soldier is going on active duty, they can notify their creditors by sending them individual orders that contain a date certain for interest calculations. This allows them to obtain interest relief during their period of active duty. This section of the SCRA says absolutely nothing about there being such a requirement for having the protections against non-judicial foreclosures or having relief from the running of a redemption period.

The defendants argued that since James never sent in his individual orders, he was not allowed to have a tolling of his redemption period. How such an argument made the illegal foreclosure legal, didn't apparently matter to them. Furthermore, he actually did send these defendants his active duty orders.

Another defense—or argument of justification the bank asserted—was that James was not liked at his cheese factory job and was about to lose his job. They claimed he would have lost the property regardless of whether he was called to active duty. A section of the SCRA discusses the applicability of some protections only if a soldier's active duty materially affects his ability to perform under a contract.

This was really a feeble-minded attempt by the bank's attorney to deflect liability for a number of reasons. First and foremost, James was loved at the cheese factory. The assertion by the bank's attorney was again an example of their willingness to take a mere scintilla of information and mold it into a completely false and fraudulent point.

The bank's attorney received information that the cheese factory owner was hostile toward James. It was true that the owner was upset with James, but not because he did not like him or felt he was bad for the company. Rather, it was because he valued James so much, and was angry that he was leaving for Iraq. The owner thought James had a choice in serving active duty and did not want him to leave.

James' coworkers loved him. Thanks to James, tragedy was once narrowly averted when the office area sustained a gas leak. While everyone ran from the premises for safety, he went in, searched the premises, and found a senior female bookkeeper had passed out, overcome with fumes. He carried her to safety and saved her from the noxious fumes. On his last day at the factory, all of the employees threw a going-away party for him complete with cakes, balloons, and an endless flow of tears. Through the five years of litigation, it was a frequent parroted expression of the bank's attorney that James was not liked at the factory, and his deployment did not materially affect his ability to pay.

As discussed, not only was this statement an outright lie, but a mischaracterization of the law. Under the SCRA, a servicemember may apply for a stay of judicial proceedings if he can show the judge that the active duty materially affects their ability to defend. The primary distinction between the law and the bank's attorney's fictitious argument is that of the non-judicial foreclosure versus a judicial foreclosure. The non-judicial proceeding against Hurley was illegal. The bank could have sought a judicial action, which would have triggered a whole new bundle of protections for Hurley, as well as remedies for the bank.

But, the defendants never sought such a proceeding. Without a judicial action, the provisions of the SCRA related to material affects are never triggered (i.e., there is not a judge to request a stay from nor let alone a judicial proceeding to get stayed). The principles are so elementary that such an argument pours salt on the wounds of the egregious acts of the defendants and then the manner in which they attempted to defend.

To even make matters worse, Judge Quist developed yet another legal fiction by ruling in accordance with the SCRA by not allowing a material affect-type analysis; but, then would allow the defendants to assert Hurley's inability to pay on the mortgage. They did not acknowledge that James had been paying on the property for the past ten years, and had only become fiscally challenged as a result of being activated. The fact that he could still make his mortgage payment while on active duty was irrelevant. Further, even if he were unable to make it while on active duty is just as irrelevant in a non-judicial foreclosure.

Such an analysis would have been appropriate in a state judicial foreclosure action, but not in the Federal Court action for the defendants' failure to comply with the SCRA. The Defendants—by their own choice, blew the opportunity to argue these issues when they chose to violate the SCRA.

Quist's decision to keep "material affect" out, yet allow Hurley's ability or inability to pay, was intellectually dishonest. The two are the same. Again, he allowed the defendants to cloud the issues and confuse the jury. There is an old trial expression: "if the law is on your side, pound the law; if the facts are on your side, pound the facts; if neither are on your side, pound the table." Quist allowed the defendants to pound the table and confuse the jury by pounding inaccurate laws and made-up facts.

He was constantly struggling with his conservatism and desire to help the banking defendants. Not only did the material affect issue not have a place in the SCRA cause of action, he was misapplying its principle. In a judicial proceeding for eviction, a soldier may present the court with the argument that their military service (active duty)

had a material affect on the ability to perform, or defend the action. Therefore, the court should adjourn the action. It was contrary to what the defendant argued and how Quist seemed to want to rule.

It was a constant uphill battle for the Hurley team. Aside from the court's challenges, the year appeared to be coming to a satisfactory end. November 15th of each year, is a sacred day for deer hunters in Michigan. It is like being a kid on Christmas morning for adults who like to deer hunt. Both James and Matt looked forward to opening day 2008. The general feeling for 2008, was that the Christmas of 2007 pleading nightmare was over. During the fall of 2007, Matt pushed as much of his caseload as he could to the back burner to work daily on nothing but Hurley pleadings. In 2008, Dan and Frank, who would affectionately come to be known as "the Italians", were now on board. Colonels Odom and Huckabee agreed to be named as experts on the court's witness list for the plaintiffs, and would help out in any way they could. The fall of 2008 looked very promising.

CHAPTER
ODOM'S MANTRA

The United States, through Congress, enacted legislation that sets forth numerous protections for our servicemembers. A stated purpose of the SCRA is to strengthen the security of the United States. The Constitutional basis under which Congress has adopted a civil relief statute for servicemembers derives from the power of Congress "to declare war" and "to raise and support armies".

In 2003, after the September 11, 2001 attacks on the United States of America and the commencement of war in Iraq, Congress overhauled the decades-old Soldiers' and Sailors' Civil Relief Act, and enacted a completely new replacement protection for servicemembers, called the "Servicemembers' Civil Relief Act", Public Law 108-189 (the "SCRA"). The SCRA was codified at 50 U.S.C. App. §§ 501-596.

The updated statute modernized the language of the Act and codified a number of matters that had been the frequent subject of litigation. It also provided several new areas of protection for servicemembers, many of which were a direct reflection of the fact that the Reserves and National Guard were being utilized in the Global War on Terror far more than in previous wars. The use of Reserves, and particularly the National Guard, in current conflicts as a strategic operating force, as opposed to a purely reserve force, was unprecedented in the history of the country.

The purpose of the SCRA, as stated in 50 U.S.C. App. § 502 is:

(1) to provide for, strengthen, and expedite the national defense through protection extended by this Act to servicemembers of the United States to enable such persons to devote their entire energy to the defense needs of the Nation; and (2) to provide for the temporary suspension of judicial and administrative proceedings and transactions that may adversely affect the civil rights of servicemembers during their military service.

The United States Supreme Court had made it perfectly clear, that deference will be given to soldiers when there is a question as to an interpretation of the Act and its application to a specific set of facts. Preferential treatment is always given in favor of the soldier. Colonel John S. Odom, Jr. played an integral part in drafting amendments to sections of the SCRA.

In addition, he is quite blunt when he responds to critics of certain sections (generally lenders trying to take advantage of a soldier) "that if you don't like what the Act states, go to Congress and get them to change it." Colonel Odom was able to say that respectfully, because he had done just that.

Few had a better understanding of the SCRA and its provisions, than Col. Odom. He developed his own mantra for SCRA cases. In response to most any argument put forth by the defense, Col. Odom simply responded with a shrug of his shoulders and said, "I don't care." Then when the critic responded "but..." Col. Odom will cut them off with, "I don't care." Very few legislative Acts are so clear and definitive in the protections that the SCRA affords soldiers.

Odom would frequently help a soldier somewhere in the United States; helping to protect their SCRA rights. A common set of facts usually involved rental storage units, car or apartment leases. He had initiated many cases, which involved home mortgages or business loans. Typically, the violations involved an administrative error that, once discovered and exposed, was resolved and the case settled. Judges around the country frequently called Odom for advice that concerned judicial proceedings in their court against an active duty servicemember.

In the Hurley case, the defendants set forth numerous defenses and assertions that were all met with Col. Odom uttering his mantra, "I don't care." When the defense stated that there was no private right of action for an SCRA case, Col. Odom declared that such a defense was "ridiculous," and, "I don't care. The court cases have clearly established an interpretation of the SCRA that makes it a well-established principle that the act provides for a private right of action."

The defendants argued that Sgt. Hurley did not send his individual orders. While he may have provided his unit orders, the Act requires individual orders for relief from a foreclosure. Colonel Odom's response was, "I don't care he didn't send his individual orders. That requirement is for the 6% cap on interest. There is no requirement for Hurley to have provided his individual orders. Further, court cases have established that the burden is on the lender to make a determination as to the truth and accuracy of their affidavit wherein they declare his military status."

The defense declared that Hurley's military service didn't affect his ability to pay the loan. Colonel Odom's response was again, "I don't care. Hurley's ability to pay the loan would relate to his ability to defend a court action. In the Hurley case, there was a non-judicial foreclosure." The defense argued that even if they had done a court action and sought judicial relief, Hurley would not have been able to obtain a loan, and his military service would not have affected his ability.

"I don't care", is the response as the defendants ignored the fact that they had denied Hurley that opportunity by moving forward with an illegal, non-judicial foreclosure. Any argument that Hurley may or may not have made in court was pure speculation, as it was the defendant's acts that deprived him of that opportunity.

The defendants made numerous arguments that attacked Hurley's ability to prove damages in his case. First, the defense argued that Hurley was upside down on his mortgage. In fact, according to the bank, they were suing him for more than $50,000, and he owed $100,000 on a house that they were only able to sell for $75,000. The defense attempted to argue that they did Hurley and his family a favor by getting him out from under the home.

In this regard, the defense added that Hurley in fact, preferred the Bangor property he lived in more, than his former Hartford river property. The defendants wrapped up this line of damage arguments by stating that it was simply a mistake on their part, and therefore no punitive damages were warranted.

The defendants made further claims that the entire fault lie with Valla and Brandie Hurley who did not properly look out for James' interest. An additional defense was laid out which stated that Hurley was not an actual combat soldier, and therefore his military service was not that much of a distraction to prevent the foreclosure and eviction. Colonel Odom's mantra could not have been more fitting for these frivolous assertions. The defense added to its strategy of delay, an element of confusion. It seemed that they had no interest in an effort to determine the truth and work toward finding justice. They simply tried to minimize their exposure in Hurley, and hide their actions of malfeasance.

The SCRA contains numerous types of protections. Regarding Hurley and the protections from creditors, careful deliberations and applications were considered which dated back to the 1860s. Absolute loan relinquishments would do more harm to soldiers than good. Creditors may altogether cease to make loans to people in the military. Congress made the obvious compromise as to what could have prevented the violations in Hurley, and that is perceived through a court action. The root for all of the problems in Hurley resulted from the defendant's illegal foreclosure. It could have all been avoided through what the SCRA allows – a court action.

When the defense argued that they felt Hurley was not entitled to a private cause of action, Odom's mantra of "I don't care", is sound. Previous case law says that it does allow for a private cause of action, and obviously Congress would not grant a right without a remedy. Regarding the defense's counter to Odom's declaration ("but Hurley did not provide *individual* orders") Odom's mantra once again applies because the requirement for providing individual orders applies to the 6% interest reduction only. There is no such requirement for any of the other sections. The burden is on the bank that executed and signed an affidavit that swore Sgt. James Hurley was *not* in the military service. Not only was he in the military through the National Guard, he was in fact on active duty.

The defense set forth its arguments concerning damages that "he actually liked his family lake cottage *better* than the river property". Col. Odom's mantra of "I don't care", again applied as the defendants took it upon themselves to make up this ridiculous fact. The SCRA allows for actual punitive damages. Congress felt that there was no better way to prevent someone from violating a servicemember's rights than to punish violators with a large damages/money fine. A large monetary award to the soldier is the punishment for violating the SCRA, and is clearly set forth within the Act.

All was finally starting to fall in place for the Hurleys. James made the cottage livable for himself and his family. Valla, Brandie, and the girls seemed to accept the loss of the river home and optimistically made the best of the cottage. Brandie and Valla became experts in mixing the mortar just right for the stone, brick, and tile work that James did around the addition.

Matt's incredible legal team included: Dan Romano in Detroit, Frank Melchiore in St. Petersburg, Florida, Col. Odom in Shreveport, Louisiana; Col. Huckabee, a law professor at the University of South Dakota, and Attorney Cordell Jones of Marcellus, Michigan. Cordell's family owns a Savings and Loan Bank that had been a part of his family for generations. He was the expert the team needed on banking and related issues such as credit scores. Cordell eventually provided expert testimony that the value of one's credit to an individual is "priceless."

Lisa Hudson, a paralegal in the Schuitmaker, Cooper, Cypher & Knotek

Law Office, was the glue that held the team together. She would eventually file (through PACER) more than 385 docket entries. For years it would seem that Lisa was on the telephone, or in communications in some manner with all the team players. Over its many years, the Schuitmaker, Cooper, Cypher & Knotek firm had many great legal assistants, but with the complexity and hostility engaged in by the defendants, Lisa was the only one that could have handled the Hurley case. She is truly exceptional, highly intelligent, and has more legal abilities than most attorneys.

The case moved along slowly in 2008. Odom's mantra kept everyone upbeat and positive. Everyone was working hard. The defendants filed a Motion for Summary Judgment based on the same argument they used when asking Edmunds to dismiss the case— that there is not an independent private cause of action under the SCRA. This was a frivolous argument. Case law said otherwise, and in this case the argument had already been considered and rejected.

***

On most Tuesdays in the summer, Matt would get out of the office, pick up his sons, and rush to the ballpark. As the assistant Coach of Bennett's baseball team, he was in charge of getting the whole roster five to ten good hits in the batting cage while the head coach worked with the infielders. On one Tuesday, just as the boys got their equipment together and prepared to jump out of the car, Matt's phone rang. It was Frank Melchiore. It was 6 p.m., and was the prime time of Frank's workday. It was a conference call and Odom was also was on the line.

After some discussion, Odom sensed Matt was not focused on the call and became irritated. Matt was serious when he said he had to pitch batting practice, but Odom did not think it was funny, nor did he understand that Matt was serious. The kids need batting practice before a game. There were six kids standing outside Matt's car staring at him, wondering when he would get off the phone.

Edmunds had already ruled on this issue. Case precedent was clear. The drafters of the SCRA (Colonel's Huckabee and Odom) both knew the Act set forth an independent private cause of action. It was simply ridiculous to think that the frivolous motion and argument could have any traction now. But, the fact that Matt had three kids, and was an assistant coach of a youth baseball team did not matter to those on the line.

For some reason they were concerned about Quist and the Motion for Summary Judgment. Frank was concerned with the judge's conservative nature, and Odom had a bad feeling that the judge did not have a good understanding of the SCRA. Matt had to get to the batting cage, so he told the guys to just stick to Odom's mantra. It is right. Quist will not get it wrong.

On September 30, 2008 Judge Quist entered an Order that dismissed the Hurley SCRA case. Surprisingly, the Hurley team took Quist's decision in stride. They all knew it was simply because Quist had a difficult time overcoming his ultra-conservative nature, and did not understand the SCRA. Once Odom could educate him, Quist would have to make the right decision. Quist was not known for being intellectually dishonest. Within the week, on October 8, 2008, the Hurley team filed a Motion for Reconsideration.

In the dismissal, Quist cited a Texas case that ruled that there was not an independent private right of action under the SCRA. Quist missed the appeal of that Texas case, the ultimate reversal, and ruling that there *is* a private right of action. Once this simple error was pointed out to him, Quist would make a correct ruling. The team sought a Motion for Reconsideration.

It had been a long year, the Hurley team needed to close it out with Quist fixing his bad decision. The August trial date set by Edmunds had long ago been forgotten. James and Matt welcomed the few days off they were going to take for the upcoming November 15 opening day of deer season. But, before Matt left the office on November 14, the PACER system indicated on docket entry #145 that Judge Quist stood by his dismissal of the Hurley SCRA claims. Judge Quist declared that the SCRA does not provide for a private cause of action.

He entered an Order to deny the Hurley's Motion for Reconsideration. Judge Quist just threw the Hurley SCRA case out.

Matt decided to wait and tell James the bad news the following week. He knew that James was going into the woods tomorrow and he certainly did not need to be thinking about what Judge Quist had done. The entire Schuitmaker, Cooper, Cypher & Knotek office was numb. Matt and Lisa did not know what to say to one another. It was simply unbelievable. Quist's opinion completely contradicted all precedent. Odom's mantra would clearly be pushed to its outer limits for this test. Odom knew Quist was wrong and his mantra would prevail, but it would simply take time.

The *Military Times* reported on Quist's decision by stating "A Michigan Federal Judge has ruled that a Soldier does not have the legal right to sue his bank for foreclosing on his property while he was on active duty." The article went on to state that, "this Federal Court case could have a devastating effect on military personnel seeking protection under the Servicemembers Civil Relief Act."

Matt started the case with the hope to help somebody, not devastate the rights of all of the men and women on active duty in the United States Military. Quist was wrong and everyone on the team knew it. But, that's where the case stood just before Christmas of 2008.

CHAPTER 17
THE NEED FOR A PRODUCTIVE JUDICIARY

While Quist dismissed the SCRA claims, fortunately for the Hurleys, Matt included a Michigan conversion count in the Hurley Complaint. Matt claimed that the bank wrongfully converted James' personal property (i.e., the floating docks, gazebo, and hunting blinds). The bank converted these items of personal property as their own. Michigan has a conversion statute that allows for treble damages, actual attorney fees and costs. Quist did not dismiss the entire Hurley case. The SCRA—the main case —was gone. While everyone was beside themselves, Odom and Huckabee knew Quist was wrong. -

James felt that his life was sinking away. He was suffering from many medical problems that were the result of his service in Iraq. While in Iraq, the way James dealt with the family crisis was to work non-stop. The continuous work and the straps from his bags caused many problems with his neck and right shoulder. The condition became a problem while he was in Iraq and only grew worse once he returned home. After a couple of surgeries on the vertebra in his neck, James finally had four discs removed, and a five-inch plate inserted on his spine behind his Adam's Apple.

He had to give up his job at Fort Custer. The doctors and Veteran's Administration declared James a service disabled Iraq war veteran. The war cost James his majestic home, and now his good health. He wondered what was the point of continuing the court action? The judge dismissed his SCRA claims. Quist's decision would affect all of the men and women in the United States Military on active duty in a very negative way. He certainly did not want to be behind a law that hurt his fellow comrades. It had been four years since his life had any normalcy to it. Now he feared the court would make him pay money to the bank for the deficiency, and sanction him for rejecting their offers of judgment.

In the Federal Court system, a trial court judge's decision is not automatically appealable. There was no way the case in the Hurley litigation team's opinion could move forward without the SCRA counts. Settlement negotiations, as difficult as the case had been to try and settle with the SCRA counts, without them there was no possible settlement. Before Quist dismissed the SCRA case the parties did not settle.

The first Settlement Conference on March 11, 2008 was a joke. Assigned to a Federal Judge in Ann Arbor, the bank's attorneys didn't even come to the courthouse. It was a specific order of the court that all parties with authority to settle be present. The bank's attorneys simply ignored the order, and didn't show with anyone with authority. The parties agreed to try and have a retired judge facilitate a settlement on August 12, 2009. Clearly, this was done as a tactic by the defense to buy time. After Quist's decision, the case was a mess.

In Federal Court, before you can appeal a judge's opinion (if any of the case survives, like the Hurley's conversion count) you have to ask the judge that rendered the decision for his permission to file an appeal. By December 12, 2008 the Hurley team filed a motion, which asked Judge Quist to allow Hurley's team to go to the 6th Circuit Court of Appeals in Cincinnati, Ohio to reverse his dismissal of the SCRA claims. In the spring of 2009, the case seemed to be in limbo. Worse than limbo, the SCRA portion was gone and it was nonsensical to proceed on the conversion claim alone.

The Hurley team anxiously awaited word about its ability to have an appeal on the SCRA dismissal. In March 2009, on its own (sua sponte), the Court/Judge Quist issued an Opinion and Order, which reversed his own decision to dismiss the SCRA count. Quist reinstated the Hurley SCRA claims. The judge was wrong when he dismissed the SCRA claims, the Hurley team knew it then and now Quist was admitting it.

Ironically, for years following Quists' reversal of himself, the Michigan Judges Handbook and other legal treatise on the subject, would cite as legal authority the *first* Quist decision, which declared that the SCRA does not provide for an independent right to a private cause of action.

Judge Quist scheduled the matter to proceed to trial and scheduled another settlement conference. Quist set the settlement conference to be held in the Federal Court in Lansing, Michigan. He was hopeful there could now be fruitful discussions and the parties could get a resolution. The Hurley team spent weeks preparing a brief and binders of documents for the Lansing Magistrate's consideration. Quist set a time-demanding deadline for the settlement package.

The Hurley team scrambled to gather everything that would be necessary for the Magistrate's productive consideration. The deadline was narrowly met. The Lansing Judge assigned the settlement conference to a magistrate from Michigan's upper Peninsula. What Quist had hoped would be one of the most productive events of the case toward its resolution, turned out to be the biggest waste of time yet.

Many people throughout society take a critical view of government workers. Most of the time it is an unfair assessment, as time and again it is seen that civil service and public servants are among the hardest working and caring individuals in society. But, when it comes to Federal judges and magistrates, the quality of society's representatives becomes very questionable. Federal judges are appointed for life. Such an appointment may effect a human being, and sometimes in quite a negative way. Fortunately, many State courts have a mandatory retirement age for judges.

The settlement conference Quist envisioned did not result in a conference or actual meeting of any type. The telephone conference call with

the magistrate, who coordinated the particulars of the proposed conference, was more like a whining therapy session to complain about
how he was selected to be involved with the case. The magistrate
won. He did not have to do anything. He didn't have to be involved
in the case. The third attempt at formal court-ordered settlement discussions simply did not take place. Hurley's team wasted hours, days,
and weeks preparing the brief and gathering documents necessary to
satisfy what the court demanded for their phantom attempt to schedule
an effective settlement conference.

The parties were unable to have meaningful settlement discussions
on their own. There certainly was a need for the court's involvement.
The Hurleys desperately wished the court would fulfill its role to help
the parties seek a resolution to this lawsuit. The defendants held stead-
fast to their position that they actually did the Hurleys a favor. Typically, plaintiffs want the case over with as quickly as possible. They
want to get on with their lives.

The defendants in this case had no better strategy than to delay, delay,
delay and confuse, confuse, confuse. It is a common strategy when
there is something to hide; to delay and confuse in hopes something
breaks. Good criminal defense attorneys have saved many clients from
prison by just putting the case off as long as possible. It is surprising
how often something breaks that changes the whole case. There is
not a reason to rush off to prison. Delay, delay, delay, and hope for a
break.

The defendants in the Hurley case had things to hide, and had a court
system that played right into their hands. None of the numerous settlement conferences were properly held or even scheduled. Judge Quist
burned valuable time and played into the defendant's strategy of delay
and confusion by fighting with the fact that he needed to be educated
in the SCRA. When the parties got together for discovery, the meetings were very unpleasant. The defense attorneys were arrogant and
condescending.

Early in the case, Matt was the only attorney for the plaintiffs. After
Valla's deposition, the bank's attorney cornered him and asked how

he could *not* agree to dismiss the case? Clearly, he could see how he brought a frivolous case. If he didn't now dismiss the case, Hurley would be hit with a big deficiency judgment and (Matt) would face federal sanctions. Based on Valla's testimony, Matt had to realize that there wasn't a case. How diametrically opposed could the parties have been in such a situation? Matt felt after Valla's testimony that the case could not have been stronger.

After Dan Romano joined the case as the team's local counsel in Detroit, the depositions of James were almost terminated due to the defense attorneys' indecent conduct. While on the record, whenever Dan would place an objection on the record, the defendant law office's lawyer would make juvenile hand puppet gestures. When Dan declared that the deposition should come to a halt for rescheduling of the deposition to be taken by video, the lawyer's hand-puppet chicanery came to an end.

Up until one month before the case went to trial, the defendant law office was represented by the hand-puppeteer. Some might think he was juvenile, disrespectful, arrogant, and condescending. The Hurley team came to affectionately refer to him as the attorney for the Defendant Law Firm. Their law office employed hundreds to do foreclosures in all eighty-three Michigan counties, processing thousands of foreclosures each week. They signed a false affidavit in the Hurley case because a foreclosure action requires an affidavit; they didn't care if it was true or false. They did not have time to waste on semantics such as the truth and accuracy of a sworn statement.

This law office sold itself to the over-burdened mortgage industry as quick and ruthless (the only way to deal with hundreds or even thousands of people who hadn't made their mortgage payments). The defendant law firm attorney had to be the way he was. He was just taking orders. Unfortunately, the attorney for the defendant law firm, and his puppeteer play was not necessary. Sergeant James Hurley did not deserve the added humiliation that the law firm's attorney gave him by being so condescending during his deposition.

The defendant law firm attorney was the one who filed a Motion for Sanctions against Matt. The Motion for Sanctions alleged that Matt made up sections of the SCRA. Now, they were going after Matt. After the magistrate found that Matt was citing the SCRA like the drafters of the SCRA, she dismissed the Motion. The law firm's attorney came up to Matt's counsel table in court and said to Matt,, "You would not know the truth if it was staring you in the face."

With this, Matt stood up and asked the attorney, "What did you say?" not believing or understanding what he just heard.

The law firm's attorney then ran out of the courtroom, down the hallway, and through another hallway to the elevators. Four U.S. Marshals stopped Matt from entering the same elevator. The Marshals weren't sure what they were witnessing, but must have been entertained by the law firm's attorney who ran down the hallways. These were just juvenile acts. The behavior and conduct was beyond anything the Hurley team lawyers had ever seen…but more was yet to come.

CHAPTER
COMING TO TERMS

Why didn't the defendants want to settle a case that seemed to present such clear violations of the Servicemembers Civil Relief Act (SCRA)? How could they come to defend their actions on such frivolous excuses? True their defense strategy had fooled Judge Quist as it related to the private right of action issue. Regardless of how ridiculous it was for him to actually rule that there was not a private cause of action, they were able to foil any attempt at meaningful settlement talks. And, they came close to actually having the case thrown out.

At one time, a figure with authority for the defendants publicly commented on the wide disparity between what the Hurleys wanted and how the defendants valued their case. It was true that the Hurleys did not want to pay money to the bank for the deficiency. That seems to be the epitome of what the defendants would say and do.

Usually when a party is so blatantly brazen and misinforms the public, they are trying to hide something. Clearly, Hurley's team needed to settle in for the long haul and come to terms with the fact this was about more than what happened to the Hurleys. There was something bigger at play here. The defendants were not as stupid as their claims and defenses would make them appear.

Aside from the frivolous legal theories already discussed, the defendants argued factual issues that would relate to damages. The defendants actually said that James liked his lake cottage better than the river home, and that Valla was doing what she thought was right for James and what the family wanted when she got rid of the river property while he was in Iraq so they could live at the Bangor cottage.

Unfortunately, for whatever unknown reason, Quist would be an accepting ear for what the defendants spewed. Once during trial motions, Quist even said "Yeah, I enjoy my lake cottage. The Hurleys probably did want the lake cottage over the river property." These defendants would lie and make things up. They were hiding something.

The Hurley Italians (Dan Romano and Frank Melchiore) were among the best trial lawyers. They are fanatical about court rules and rules of evidence. They are tenacious, smart, and quick on their feet. Dan and Frank came to know each other through their association with the Michigan Association for Justice (MAJ); an association of Plaintiff's Trial Attorneys in Michigan. The two worked on numerous projects and cases together over the years, and both were young men in their early forties. Physical fitness and healthy eating were life priorities for them both. They were lean, mean fighting machines that could outlast and out try anyone, hands down.

Matt was introduced to Dan through Frank. After the case was moved to Grand Rapids, everyone was happy to keep Dan on the case. The Hurley team needed all of the help it could get. The bank and the mortgage servicing company would go through no less than thirty-five attorneys throughout the case. Why would the bank go through so many lawyers? That was a head scratcher. Surely they were paying good money.

The attorneys for the bank, from the start to the end, were always steered by one woman. She was unrealistic and the author of many of their unrealistic defenses (i.e., the individual orders argument). This one attorney consistently steered the bank's defense, but she went through five law firms, and many of their attorneys put her defense plans into action. It simply made no sense. Six months before trial, the woman who lead the bank's defense pulled back and allowed the firm and attorneys that tried the case to take over. One month before trial, Puppet Guy pulled out and hired new trial counsel.

Leading up to trial, Dan and Frank took the depositions of many employees with the Mortgage Servicing Company in Texas. The depositions Frank and Dan conducted in Texas really did a lot for the Hurley case. Representatives from the Mortgage servicing company would provide testimony for how the foreclosure process commenced in the Hurley case.

The United States Department of Defense runs a website for creditors that want to determine the status of debtors with the military. Back in 2004, a creditor with access to the site, could literally in 2.5 seconds, determine Sgt. Hurley's active duty status. The Hurley team always knew that the Hurleys notified the defendants of James' legal status. Valla saved the fax confirmation slips where she faxed her son's orders to the defendants. Not until the Texas depositions of the mortgage-servicing representatives, was it confirmed that the defendants knew of Sgt. Hurley's active duty status.

The defendants knew that fact in September of 2004, when the false affidavit was signed stating otherwise. They knew in 2005 when they commenced eviction proceedings. After the running of the redemption period, which never really ran, they knew of Sgt. Hurley's active duty and that the foreclosure was illegal. The affidavit was false. Their eviction was illegal, and they knew all of this when they wrongfully sold his property two months before he came back from Iraq.

Testimony and documentation showed that these defendants had in place, an internal policy that violated the SCRA. A large foreign bank that received taxpayer bail out funds had in place a policy that violated the federally protected rights of U.S. servicemembers. Through the Texas depositions in the summer of 2010, it became clear what these defendants did to James—and what they did and are doing to hundreds if not thousands of servicemembers.

Odom was instrumental in educating Quist on the SCRA. Typically, experts in court cases are helpful in educating the fact finder on certain technical or scientific aspects of a certain situation. Judges interpret and follow the law. Clearly on an SCRA case, Col. Odom was invaluable in educating the court. He had taught at numerous judicial conferences across the country where he educated judges from across the nation. He was named as one of Hurley's experts.

Now that the SCRA claims were back on the table, it seemed that the case was back on track. Christmastime however, was always a bench mark for the progress of the Hurleys' loss and claims. It started during Christmas of 2004 when James departed for Iraq, and continued during the same in 2005, when he hoped to have his home back. Back then, Matt felt by Christmas 2006 the claims would be honored and resolved without the filing of a lawsuit. Claims were made, ignored, and the lawsuit was filed.

Given Judge Edmunds' initial assessment and admonishments to the defendants, a settlement before Christmas 2007, while slim, was hopeful. By Christmas 2008, the team prepared for a long drawn-out campaign. It was then that Matt enlisted Frank Melchiore to be Brandie's attorney, and for Dan Romano to stay on board. Colonels Odom and Huckabee agreed to provide expert opinions on the SCRA. Attorney Cordell Jones, President and CEO of the Jones Bank, was retained to provide valuable expert testimony regarding the negative affects of credit reports and ratings.

For the Hurley team, Christmas 2008 was spent sitting on their hands because of Quist's dismissal of the SCRA claims. It seemed like all was lost and years of fighting and heart ache lay ahead. Quist's reversal in early 2009 seemed invigorating, and they all felt that the case was finally going in the right direction. It was always short-lived however, given the defendants' tactics and Quist's rulings. In Quist's reversal, there was the ruling that the defendants did indeed violate the SCRA, both §526 and §533. The non-judicial foreclosure was illegal and there was a violation to not toll the redemption period. Oddly, Quist deemed the eviction to be legal even though it was obtained through fraud.

By Christmas 2009, the Hurley team was sitting on their hands again as the case was stayed while the defendant law firm appealed a ruling that Quist made relating to their request to move the case to binding arbitration. After two and a half years, the defendants made a motion and asked that the case be removed from the Federal District Court and set for binding arbitration...typical of the defense strategy of delay and confusion. Given Quist's denial, the defendants were left to seek appeal of the decision to the 6th Circuit Court of Appeals in Cincinnati, Ohio.

A mortgage agreement with a financial institution typically sets forth a binding arbitration provision that addresses resolution of disputes among the parties. It highlights what forum will be utilized as the parties agree to submit their disputes to binding arbitration. While Sgt. Hurley purchased his residence in Hartford, Michigan on September 26, 1994, on September 30, 2003 he received a loan in the amount of $95,200 and executed a mortgage on the property as security for the loan. As part of the mortgage documents, he executed a rider entitled Arbitration of Disputes stating:

All disputes, claims, or controversies arising from or related to the loan evidenced by the Note ("the Loan"), including statutory claims, shall be resolved by binding arbitration, and not by court action, except provided under [specified exclusions]. This arbitration agreement is made pursuant to a transaction involving interstate commerce, and shall be governed by the Federal Arbitration Act (9 U.S.C. §§ 1-14).

The original mortgagor was no longer a party to the agreement, but the present parties would be covered within the subsequent assignments. The defendant law firm lawyers argued that they were, as agents of the mortgagor, able to prevail themselves of the arbitration clause. Quist ruled that the defendants sat on their rights and waived their ability to make such a demand. After two and a half years of litigating a case in court, they could not now make such a request.

They had sat on the right to make a request that should have been made in the spring of 2006, immediately after being notified of a potential suit. It was certainly not permissible after numerous dispositive motions. Essentially, the defendants took the fight on in court, and having lost in their attempts to throw the case out, they wanted to get out of the system.

On April 26, 2010, Matt and Frank traveled to Cincinnati, Ohio to appear before the 6th Circuit Court of Appeals. On April 27, they went before the United States Court of Appeals for the Sixth Circuit, which covers appeals from Federal Courts in Kentucky, Michigan, Ohio, and Tennessee. They each presented for their respective clients before the court. The defendants hired appellant counsel that specialized in arguing before the Federal Appeals Court. Little did the appellate attorney realize, the defendants were setting him up to be fed to the wolves.

He knew nothing about the case; other than the arbitration clause issue. Keeping in mind the defendants waited two-and-a-half years to file a request for removal (which normally is filed within days of receiving a Complaint), the beat down he received from the Court of Appeals panel was not unexpected. Aside from the delay issue, an arbitration agreement in a mortgage has nothing to do with a SCRA claim. Hurley was not suing because the defendants violated a term of the mortgage contract.

The Hurley case was a SCRA violation case. An independent cause of action was due to the defendants' violations of a Federal Act. To allow the defendants to assert a provision of the contract, an arbitration clause would make the Federal Act null and void. Federal courts examine arbitration language in a contract in light of the strong federal policy in favor of arbitration. Any doubts as to the parties' intentions are resolved in favor of arbitration, there are no contractual intentions involved when a soldier has his or her rights violated under the SCRA.

While some states allow non-judicial foreclosures, the SCRA only permits a foreclosure against an active duty servicemember to proceed judicially. In a state that allows for non-judicial foreclosures, the bank proceeds without a court action. The bank does not invoke an arbitration rider either; it merely proceeds in accordance with the state's summary proceeding, non-judicial laws. What happens to the arbitration clause?

If Sgt. Hurley had somehow become aware of the non-judicial fore-closure, his only recourse would have been to initiate a court action to use the SCRA as a shield and get a court order to stop the non-judicial proceeding against him. Had he sought arbitration under an arbitration clause, it could not have stopped the foreclosure.

The SCRA is a federal act with specific rights and remedies and has nothing to do with the contract (whether it is a mortgage or an auto lease). A lawsuit to enforce SCRA rights is just that, a case to seek to address the violations of a servicemembers' SCRA rights. It is not, to quote the arbitration clause in Hurley, "a dispute, claim or controversy arising from or related to the loan." The plaintiff's rights under a federal act "to provide for, strengthen, and expedite the national defense of our Nation" have nothing to do with his contract with a bank. The lawyers he sued were not even parties to the contract.

His dependent (i.e., Brandie), who has an independent cause of action/ rights under the SCRA, was not even a party to the note and mortgage. How can a non-party to a contract be subject to its terms? The beat down by the Sixth Circuit Court of Appeals was as refreshing as it was to have Judge Edmunds state her position in the first hearing on the case in Detroit so long ago. She stated that the Defendants were wrong and should settle this case fast.

The panel's utter disgust with the defendants appeal was exhila-rating. Why couldn't Judge Quist see how horrible these defendants and their tactics were? The 6th Circuit simply could not believe how contrary the defendant's positions were to the case law on arbitra-tion clauses and the time delays. The defendants' flawed request to arbitrate beyond the time issue was exacerbated by their multiple motions to dismiss and for summary judgment. A party waives its ar-bitration rights after it chooses to participate in the court forum.

These defendants were now trying to get out of the judicial system because they didn't like how the court was ruling. Generally, the court gives a party one shot at a dispositive motion. The defendants in the Hurley case filed no less than five dispositive motions.

In a nutshell, the pleadings in the Hurley case were as follows:

May 2, 2007: Plaintiffs filed their complaint in the Eastern District of Michigan.

September 20, 2007: Defendants filed their answers, and the court held a Rule 16 Scheduling Conference. Plaintiffs subsequently filed an amended complaint, and defendants again filed answers.

December 10, 2007: Defendant law firm filed a motion to dismiss and for partial summary judgment.

February 12, 2008: The district court granted in part, and denied in part, the law firm's motion to dismiss.

March 3, 2008: Defendant Deutsche Bank filed a motion to change venue, in which Defendant law firm joined.

April 1, 2008: While the Bank's motion to change venue was pending, Plaintiffs filed their own motion for summary judgment.

April 17, 2008: The court granted Defendants' motion and transferred the case to the Western District of Michigan. After the transfer, Defendants filed motions for summary judgment, a motion to strike Plaintiffs' expert, a motion for sanctions and several other motions.

September 30, 2008: The district court ruled on each of these motions, granting in part and denying in part, both Plaintiffs' and Defendants' motions for summary judgment.

March 13, 2009: After denying Plaintiffs' motion for reconsideration, the court sua sponte reconsidered its September 30, 2008 order.

April 21, 2009: The court denied Defendant Deutsche Bank's motion for reconsideration.

May 21, 2009: Defendant law firm filed a motion to compel arbitration.

June 23, 2009: The district court denied the motion, holding that Defendants had waived their right to enforce the arbitration clause by sleeping on their arbitration rights for twenty-six months while Plaintiffs incurred the costs of this litigation.

July 22, 2009: Defendant law firm timely filed a notice of appeal. Defendant Deutsche Bank did not join the appeal. The Court of Appeals affirmed Quist's decision concerning the arbitration issues.

The District Court found:

To paraphrase O.J. Distributing, Defendants slept on their rights for twenty-six months while Plaintiffs incurred costs to pursue their claims in this forum and suffered prejudice. In fact, this case is in its late stages and, but for the parties' agreement to facilitative mediation, would have been set for trial within the next few months. If there were no waiver under these circumstances, it would be difficult to imagine when a waiver might occur.

Defendants have not only responded to actions taken by Plaintiffs, but they have filed multiple dispositive and non-dispositive motions of their own, including motions to dismiss, motions for summary judgment, and a motion to change venue. By filing a motion to change venue, Defendants pro-actively selected the forum in which they wished to defend against Plaintiffs' claims. As the district court found:

Although this case has been pending in this district for about fifteen months, it dates back to May 2, 2007, when Plaintiffs filed suit in the Eastern District of Michigan. Thus, it has been pending twenty-six months, during which time Orlans filed two dispositive motions, joined in Deutsche Bank's motion for change of venue, attended a Rule 16 scheduling conference and a settlement conference, and filed numerous other motions and documents in defense of Plaintiffs' claims.

Although Orlans had the mortgage documents since the inception of the lawsuit, it took no action to assert its alleged right to arbitrate until after the Court issued an unfavorable decision in its March 13, 2009, Opinion and Order.

Now the parties were looking at Christmas 2010. The Hurley team was hopeful that this would all be coming to an end very soon. Up until this time, the case received some very good national attention. The *Military Times* did a story, and in 2009, Adam Hochberg of *National Public Radio,* did a feature interview with Matt and James. There was great appreciation and excitement in the days after the *NPR* feature. After listening to Hochberg's interview, Senator Hillary Clinton held a press conference to elaborate on her concerns for soldiers who had such an experience. Folks who heard about the Hurley case were slow to react because it all seemed like such an absurdity. As a result, some U.S. banks tried to comply with the SCRA and previous offending institutions tried to reconcile problems and resolve violations.

Matt thanked goodness for Col. Odom who was not just educating the court, but for his contacts in Washington, D.C. and New York. He felt the Hurley team, U.S. Servicemembers, and America, had Col. Odom to thank for blowing the lid off the mortgage industry, which violated servicemembers' rights. The Colonel's contacts had helped ignite the National News Media and the U.S. Department of Justice onto the news of the Hurley case.

The *New York Times* sent a news crew to Paw Paw, Michigan who took video of James and the Hartford property for a story they posted on their website. On January 27, 2011, the *New York Times'* print edition featured the Hurley case on the front page. Finally the Hurley travesty and his story was getting the attention that it needed to expose the financial industry's flawed SCRA policies that surely had negatively impacted the lives of other servicemembers.

James' dream house and property was gone forever, as the current owner refused to sell it. The new owner had in fact, legally purchased the property from the bank, and was an innocent party to the transaction. The property was out of reach in the case. The new owner refused to sell even when Matt offered him one million dollars for the property during his deposition in Chicago. The new owners were good people; they simply wanted to be left alone to enjoy the property that they innocently purchased.

A week after the *New York Times* article, Matt's teenage daughter, Anella, was thumbing through *People Magazine*. There in her swimsuit was Katie Couric, poolside, reading the *New York Times*. The photo clearly depicted that Couric was reading the edition with Hurley on the front page. Within a week, a *CBS Evening News* crew was in Paw Paw. Trial was scheduled to begin in a month and the media was getting involved.

Katie Couric ran a *CBS Evening News* feature story with General Petraeus and his wife, Holly. Holly was getting heavily involved with servicemembers and their financial woes during the collapse of the U.S. Housing and mortgage foreclosure crisis. She was out to protect servicemembers from predatory creditor tactics. The Hurley story blended perfectly with the Petraeus storyline. The staff of Diane Sawyer and the *ABC Nightly News* soon contacted Matt. The CBS network had a crew who shot video and worked on the story with Matt and James for more than a week.

Leading up to the airtime, The *ABC* network was working on a similar story and wanted to include the Hurley case. One afternoon Matt was on his cell phone with the CBS staff when the ABC staff called on his office line. The call was put through and Matt placed CBS on hold to take ABC's call. The national media's concern for such an important issue was beyond the Hurley team's hopes and expectations. Both networks ran the story.

That weekend, James and Matt were on *Fox and Friends Live*. Early on a Saturday morning, the two, along with Matt's youngest son Bennett, traveled through a snowstorm to a news studio in Grand Rapids. Laurie was working at her nursing job that weekend, their daughter Anella was away at University, and their son Drew, was staying with friends.

At the Fox studios, Matt did not want Bennett out of his sight and alone in the green room while they were live on television. The news crew allowed Bennett to stand just a few feet away from the stage so that Matt could keep an eye on him. Matt told Bennett that when he touched his chin, he was telling him, "I love you."

Going live on national television was very stressful for James and Matt, but they were fighting a good cause and they made themselves do it. The secret, silent communication between Matt and Bennett allowed his youngest son to share in some of the excitement of the situation.

The New York Times article catapulted the Hurley case into newspapers around the world—all except the local paper in Paw Paw. *The Malaysian Sun* ran numerous stories, which poked fun at the United States. The Malaysians questioned how the world's super power could send soldiers overseas to fight in a war and allow a foreign bank to illegally take his home? Congressional offices called to invite Matt and James to Washington, D.C. to give testimony.

Regrettably, many of the numerous requests for news interviews could not be fulfilled. James and Matt really wanted to accept being on *Inside Edition* with Debra Norvill, but the trial date was quickly approaching, and the Congressional hearings were scheduled the same week that the trial commenced.

Unbeknownst to the others in the Hurley team, Col. Odom had reached out to people he knew in the United States Department of Justice. As the trial approached, Col. Odom had informed them that the Department of Justice had been tracking their case for the past two years. -

TRIAL MAY FINALLY COME

When Col. Odom came to Paw Paw, it had been his second time ever in Michigan. He and his wife Gayle Johnson Odom Ph.D., loved to travel. Gayle was the Dean of the Hurley School of Music at Centenary College of Louisiana, and was an internationally acclaimed opera singer who performed in the popular movie, *Steal Magnolias*. Many years ago, after the couple traveled to Chicago for a Cubs game, the two traveled north through Wisconsin, across Michigan's Upper Peninsula, and then south through Michigan.

The trip through Michigan was done for the sake of being able to say, that they traveled through Michigan. To the folks from the South, one northern woods—whether Wisconsin, Michigan, or Maine for that matter—seemed like the other. The Odoms were from a land where Azaleas and Magnolias are in full bloom when northern folks are still shoveling snow. The Odoms had traveled the world from African Safaris to escapades throughout Europe.

Colonel Odom, as a licensed attorney, also had handled cases all over the United States. Michigan did not particularly set itself out to him. In fact, during his opening statement in the Hurley case, he referred to Bangor, Michigan as Bangor, *Maine*. Physically he could have been anywhere. His mind was on the SCRA and the protections it afforded to servicemembers.

Every year, at the time of year the colonel was settling in Grand Rapids for the Hurley Trial, numerous friends gathered at the Odom home to watch Mardi Gras parades. Instead, he was traveling to the part of the country that he liked the least—and at the time of year he detested most. Cold and snow did not set well with the fair-skinned Southern Cajan (or Southern Gentlemen depending to whom he was talking). He was larger than life, and could be everything in between, from drafter of the SCRA amendments to Mardi Gras host.

For example, when he worked at the Pentagon, he received a very high security clearance. The Federal government issued him an identification badge that included his security clearance level. Federal courthouses have very strict security, and are protected by United States Marshals. Courthouse entry is restricted to one point of access, and it is quite a process to be scanned and cleared for entry. The process is repeated regardless of how many times in a day an individual comes and goes.

One day, after frequent visits to the Federal Courthouse in Grand Rapids, Col. Odom inquired as to the routine. A U.S. Marshal sarcastically quipped, "Not unless you have a clearance by the United States Government." Colonel Odom never went through the screening again. The Marshals became quite familiar with him after that. While everyone else would slowly work their way through the long single-file line, Col. Odom would be recognized from a distance and waived through. Typically, he would be waiting at the end of the checkpoint exchanging southern recipes with his new-found friends from the north, and U.S. Marshal Service. One day in particular, they were especially grateful for the fax they received from his office with his secret Louisiana Gumbo recipe.

His new friends almost helped him forget his first trip to Michigan for the case. It was during a treacherous drive through a snowstorm from Chicago. After Col. Huckabee's deposition in a conference room at the O'Hare Airport, Matt drove the colonel to Paw Paw. It had been quite a productive trip. Who better to have such incredulous and disingenuous defendants depose than the colonel that named the Act and was one of Plaintiffs' SCRA experts? After all, Col. Huckabee had been assigned to update and rename the Soldiers' and Sailors' Civil Relief Act by President Taft's great grandson, General Taft. The news media initially labeled this case a David and Goliath type conflict. The best thing Matt could have ever done was to involve Col. Odom, whose contacts proved priceless.

After a white-knuckled trip from Chicago to Paw Paw through a Midwestern snowstorm, Col. Odom experienced more snow than he had in his lifetime (and never hoped to encounter again). For the first time in his life, he personally experienced that oddly phrased expression "lake effect snow." The staff at Matt's office loved the energy he brought with his visits.

On his first visit, Matt took him to the former Hurley home in Hartford, through Bangor, and to the courthouse in South Haven. Matt introduced him to Judge Clarke and showed him the jury room that the defendants' attorney used to hide Valla away from the court and Judge Clarke. Clearly from their meetings with Judge Clarke, the defendants intended to perpetrate a fraud on the court so that they could get the Hurleys off the property and sell the home. On so many occasions, the possibility of saving James' home was undone by the defendants' reprehensible conduct. If the law could have been followed—or even if the progressive steps to circumvent it had not been followed—James would have never lost his home.

Colonel Odom was surprised that the snow-covered roads were in fact plowed, and that this was the roadway fit for travel. For lunch, they ate at the Maple Grove Tavern in Van Buren County. The bar and grill was so interesting to the new visitor, that he couldn't help but take photos of the small establishment with such a large crowded bar. In addition, it served one of the best Bacon Blue Cheese Burgers he had ever had.

The history-making trial was going to be an experience of a lifetime for a man who had dedicated his professional life to the protections of U.S. Servicemembers. His mantra of, "I don't care" is only topped by his insistence that if the defendants do not like what he says, they should go to Congress and change it. That is what he did; help make the SCRA what it should be. Congress had always sought protections for its servicemembers, and the courts were to interpret the law in factual situations with an eye friendly toward the benefit of servicemembers.

The Supreme Court has declared that there is to be preferential treatment and review with deference toward soldiers. Hence, the Odom Mantra and his morning trial ritual of singing "we are going to kick some ass today." What better cause to take up than the protection of the U.S. Servicemember?

The Hurley Team felt honored and obligated to fight for the Hurley cause and expose what some financial institutions were doing to servicemembers. To Odom, it made no difference if he was in Bangor, Maine or Bangor, Michigan. He had no idea of the difference between Michigan State or the University of Michigan. However, he was there and ready for service in the Hurley battle on the home front.

Frank Melchiore's travel to Michigan was much less of an upheaval to him. Originally from Chicago, he had worked for ten years in a prominent victims' rights firm in Michigan. Frank frequently traveled back to Michigan, and it was a common bet between Matt and Frank, who could get to Detroit the fastest (Matt's driving or Frank's flying in from Tampa)? More often than not, the flight from Tampa would arrive at the airport in Detroit before Matt was there to pick him up.

The two enjoyed the years they worked on cases together. They realized early that it was necessary to have separate counsel for Brandi and James. Their marriage had suffered greatly through the stress of the foreclosure. Admirably, James never blamed Valla or Brandie for what happened even though a common tactic of the defendants was to try and play the blame game with one, or all of them. Ultimately, none of them could have done anything differently given the illegal and fraudulent conduct of the defendants.

The Hurley trial team was camped out on the 21st floor of a condominium sky rise, which overlooked downtown Grand Rapids. It was a long walk, much too long of a walk in the bitter cold of March 2011. On most trial days, the team traveled the short drive in Matt's car.

Dan Romano drove in from Detroit every day. Valla and James commuted each day from Bangor. Matt's foresight for having separate legal counsel for Brandie was spot on, given that she was now living in Texas. For the trial, she would stay with her friend in a hotel in Grand Rapids.

While Quist reversed his dismissal of the SCRA counts, he was a constant problem for the plaintiffs. In a footnote in the opinion that Quist wrote reinstating the SCRA claims, he took away the Hurley's ability to seek punitive damages. Essentially while he was giving the Hurleys their case back, he was limiting the value of the case. It seemed as though he was forcing himself to do the right thing, but was not going to allow the Hurleys to get something he did not want them to have.

Judge Quist had his own opinions of the SCRA contrary to our Supreme Court directing deference to a soldier's rights. Congress has enacted legislation through the SCRA that gave soldiers protections— as both a shield and a sword—that the country should be proud of. However, in the banking capitol of the Midwest, in front of a conservative Republican federal judge, one certainly would not have thought that the Hurley team was representing a soldier; particularly one that had his home illegally taken by a foreign bank *while* he was serving his country in a war in Iraq. It was a constant uphill battle with Judge Quist whose ruling on punitive damages benefitted the defendants. His proposed jury instructions played right into the defense's strategy.

Between December 22 and 23, 2010 the defendants filed Motions in Limine to:

Preclude testimony that the manufactured home was personalty and testimony that it was allegedly converted after March 15, 2005;

Exclude statements or references to James Hurley's temporary duty orders as qualifying for SCRA Relief;

Exclude Plaintiff James Hurley's proffered expert Cordell Jones;

\# Exclude Plaintiffs' proffered experts Colonels Gregory Huckabee and John S. Odom, Jr.;

\# Exclude all evidence and references to the Sixth Circuit Court of Appeals July 1, 2010 opinion;

\# Exclude all evidence and references to plaintiffs' alleged damages from impaired credit;

\# Exclude all evidence and references to the eviction proceedings or alleged fraud;

\# Exclude all evidence and references to bank bailouts, foreclosure volumes, foreclosure proceedings, and similar references;

\# Exclude all evidence and references to plaintiffs' alleged medical and emotional damages;

\# Exclude all testimonial and documentary evidence and references to (1) communications relating to whether and when Mr. Hurley qualified for SCRA protection; and (2) punitive damages.

These motions now had to be fought after years of numerous dispositive motions, which sought complete dismissals and appeals. There was no judicial control or oversight on the Hurley case. This was an important case, which involved the rights of soldiers, the consequences of the mortgage crisis, and crash of the housing market over active duty personnel. In addition, it was being exposed through a David versus Goliath legal team, which involved one of the world's largest banks, and now had to prosecute the case in what seemed a banking-friendly judicial system.

Christmas 2010 brought the regular defense delay, delay, delay tactic to an agreeable court. The January 2011 trial date was pushed back to March. Push did come to shove and the court would not continue to duck the case. The case went through four Federal judges and two magistrates. Just weeks before the original January trial date, Judge Quist granted a defense motion, which concerned the use of Hurley's SCRA experts.

He was not going to allow Colonels Odom and Huckabee to be called as witnesses. These experts had military background and could help the jury understand the effects active duty had on a soldier, and the damages a soldier experienced when his SCRA rights were violated and exploited. Their expert testimony would aid the jury in understanding active duty orders and the mechanics around deployments. Both men are professional, well spoken and animated speakers.

Their testimony was planned to be moving and riveting. Matt and Frank were counting on the two to simplify the SCRA for the jury. They also counted on the men to move the jury (in a very patriotic way) to show its love for its soldiers and America by bringing back a large punitive award to Hurley. Punitive damages are all about emotions, and what better way to tell a defendant that what you did was wrong, than punitive damages? Punitive damages exist to punish violators. Corporations cannot go to prison so they have to be hit where they feel it…in the pockets.

Voir dire jury selection would be especially critical in this case. Damage assessment in this case, and the ultra conservative nature of Grand Rapids and its jury pool, would require careful jury selection. Conservatives and Republicans in general are anti-lawsuits. As far as they were concerned, injury claims should be non-existent, except when it involved one of their own.

Of even more significant danger in jury selection is the large number of Christian Reformed in Grand Rapids. Among many in Grand Rapids, there is a common belief that compensating someone for their suffering is offensive, and belittles the suffering. Suffering cannot be that bad if it can be alleviated with money. The victory comes from a positive verdict, not in the amount sought. To them, a person's real reward would come in the next life. Obviously, the Hurley team was going to be very involved in Voir Dire and jury selection.

Just before the trial commenced, Docket Entry #141 is Judge Quist's decision to strike Colonel Odom, and Docket Entry #324 to strike Huckabee as expert witnesses. He then determined through Docket

Entry #242 that neither Sgt. Hurley nor his wife Brandie, are entitled to punitive damages. Judge Quist determined that there would be no direct participation by the attorneys in the Voir Dire process; even though attorneys are *always* involved in Voir Dire. Whose side was he on? He even ruled that the eviction was legal. Wonderful!

Quist had reluctantly given Hurley his SCRA claims back, but now he was going to make sure the Hurleys couldn't win, or at the very least get a small financially positive award. In footnote #3 in Quist's 8-13-2009 Opinion, Judge Quist indicated "the Bank offered evidence that James Hurley had the ability to make his mortgage payment but elected to stop making payments on the property several months before the foreclosure might be relevant to the issue of damages. The bank's proximate cause argument (which pertains to all types of damages) essentially makes his point.

Because this argument was not presented in a timely filed Motion for Summary Judgment, the court would now consider it. The bank may present such evidence at Trial." In this footnote he goes on to discuss Hurley's ability to pay, and the defendant's ability to use that as a defense. This footnote illustrates his appalling lack of understanding of the purpose of prohibiting non-judicial foreclosures. Such analysis of the issue only pertains to a court action.

Clearly the defendants cannot use this in the present case. In this trial, the ability of Hurley to have paid the mortgage is irrelevant. However, the judge made it relevant as to damages. He was making wrong decisions in favor of the defendants. First he threw the case out and reluctantly let it back in, but ham-stringed the plaintiffs so they would not be able to prove a case; and if they did, it would allow minimal compensation. Judge Quist had prevented the plaintiffs from having the jury hear from their expert witnesses. He had completely overlooked and disregarded the need, importance, and significance of having the jury hear from military experts.

Up to this point, Col. Odom was the most important private practice SCRA attorney in the country. Now, he was just struck from one of the most important cases involving the SCRA. Hurley's case was going to be the first time the SCRA would be put in front of a jury. He was exposing what would become the tip of the iceberg for violations against servicemembers during the foreclosure crisis in our country. Sometimes it felt that the fight was with Judge Quist, not the defendants. The Federal judge, who all the case law directs to err on the side of caution for our soldiers, seemed to look at the Hurley case in reverse, just as when he decided to overturn case law, which referenced the mere applicability of the SCRA to Hurley.

It had been five years since Matt had taken on the Hurley case. These defendants (and what appeared to be with the help of the judge) were now going to prevail in a matter where the defendants were clearly wrong. The case had entered its home stretch. Plaintiffs' attorneys, in general accident type cases, feel the dichotomy of the political parties. Republicans play into insurance companies and business interests. Democrats play into victim's rights and the injured. Quist, as a conservative Republican, and with a Dutch Christian Reformed Church background, was driving home all of the stereotypes.

After all the national news media, the trial team was contacted by military groups and other people who took an interest in the case. Virg Bernaro, Mayor of Lansing, Michigan and former candidate for Governor, frequently called Matt as the trial approached. The two did not personally know one other, nor had they ever met, but Bernaro had read and heard about the Hurley case in the media. Mayor Bernaro provided much-needed words of encouragement as a community leader. Frequently, the Mayor would say supporting Hurley is not about being a Democrat or a Republican. It is about being an American. On the other hand, Republicans, whom Matt considered personal friends, would shun the case and encourage Matt to stay quiet about the issues in the media.

The Hurleys had come this far and dealt with so much; Judge Quist would not be a source of their downfall. If Quist was not going to let Col. Odom testify as a witness, Matt, Frank, and Dan decided to have him join the trial team as one of their attorneys. In that role, he would instruct the jury about the SCRA and active duty, through an opening statement and other witness examinations. On December 6, 2010, Docket Entry #240, Colonel John S. Odom, Jr., filed his Appearance as co-counsel for James B. Hurley. The Hurley team was not going to lose to the defendants' frivolous defenses and claims, or a Federal judge's improper predispositions and rulings.

The state and federal judiciary (just like any other vocation) has some really great jurists as well as some bad apples. The best judges you find typically are individuals that have sought out the judiciary after extensive legal experience and community service. This includes attorneys who have actually been in practice and have accomplished something. Far too often, the bad apples are simply lazy political hacks. Some judges take the job for an easy paycheck. They were failures as practicing attorneys and the pay is better than they ever imagined to make as an attorney.

Some get the job because of who their parents are/were. As Justice Weaver said, "Keep an eye on the Incompetents." How well does she, and others like her, serve our community when murderers go free because of what happens in her courtroom? It is generally just like anything else; a microcosm of society, where life is not always fair. There are good ones and bad ones.

If one thinks about it, it really becomes a concern that our country really is not that old. Modern-day society for our country is still truly in its infancy. Justice Weaver, former Chief Justice of the Michigan Supreme Court, asserts in her book *Judicial Deceit*, that our situation is "Noah-like." It is time to get on the Ark. If there is not attention given to our judges (the third branch of our government), the judiciary and our country, is truly in trouble.

Is Michigan different or the prime example? There was a time in Michigan during the height of the automotive industry that it was the land of milk and honey. There was a quid pro quo between the legislature and the judicial system that related to the money that was filling the coffers of the legislature and the judiciary. Thankfully, Michigan was able to have term limits imposed upon the career politicians in Michigan. In fact, Michigan has a part-time legislature.

However, even today these representatives of the public get paid as though they are full-time employees with massive office budgets and staff. The Michigan Legislature is the second highest paid in the nation. Most states have true part-time legislatures. This culture transcends to the judiciary given the political involvement in judicial selection at both the Federal and State court level.

It is all part of the political culture. Does Michigan really need to send a bunch of part-time legislatures on a junket to Israel? Imagine how productive it is for the interest of the people of the State of Michigan to have your representative attend a conference in the Pacific Northwest or Southern California. Michigan needs to follow up its move to term limits with making the part-time status of its legislative branch a reality.

The massive expenditure of staff and cost perks, and a reduction in their full-time salary to truly reflect their part-time effort would be an enormous infusion into the state budget. Most states in the country do not have the fictions of office seen in Michigan. How does Michigan government rank among all of the other states? Check with the National Center for Public Integrity; particularly relating to transparency, accountability and ethics. Frequently, Michigan is at the bottom. Michigan voters would surely pass a measure for a part-time legislature.

It is not uncommon to see a judge in Michigan retire after fifteen years of service, only to receive a retirement payment at about 60% of their normal salary, and then take another government job; essentially allowing them to double-dip. While legislatures collect their retirement and become lobbyists, the public has tried to address it through term limits. However, the judiciary is ignored.

As retired Chief Justice Weaver has expressed, there is need for reform in the Michigan Judiciary. It is quite harsh words to state that the Michigan Judicial System is corrupt. It seems the main problem from

District, Circuit, and Court of Appeals Judges to Supreme Court Justices is the appointment process. The governor is given Carte Blanche on what he wants to do. There is no meaningful application process or review prior to the governor's appointment. The Michigan Bar does have a Judicial Qualifications Committee that has a very dedicated board that seriously undertakes their responsibilities. The membership dedicates numerous hours, effort, and energy into their position on the qualifications committee. Unfortunately, they have no say with the governor. Colorado is said to have a model system. They have a committee similar to the Michigan Judicial Qualifications Committee that plays a role in the selection process.

Michigan's reform should have a productive selection process. Independent scholars and assessment organizations have consistently ranked Michigan as the worst judiciary in the country. Surely with Justice Weaver's disclosures, there are serious-needs for reform. Justice Weaver blames a lot of the political mess on former Governor John Engler. It is asserted that current Governor Snyder is simply "Engler in sheep's clothing." Her book goes on to allege that Snyder probably does not even know the error of his ways.

Unfortunately, for Snyder, he does not have the political acumen of Governor Engler; and therefore, some day his true character will be exposed. Sadly, Snyder has filled his administration with the political trouble- makers behind Engler's administration. He has allowed those that he has designated to a position of authority to make their own decisions. Unfortunately, there are many that he has trusted that he probably should not. For example, Snyder's Judicial Appointments Officer has continued to make appointments that Weaver has pointed out are a complete disservice to our community and the Michigan Judiciary.

Judge Quist of course is a Federal judge, and these reforms would not affect his lifetime appointment. It is however, about the judicial culture in our country. Abraham Lincoln once said, "Nearly all men can stand adversity, but if you want to test a man's character, give him power." Both of these statements came into play when Judge Quist denied the Motion for Reconsideration. Matt's and James' characters would truly be measured, given that they were facing an opinion that not only defied the law, but also logic. The one in power had set the law protecting the rights of our servicemembers on its head.

A must read is the book written by former Michigan Supreme Court Chief Justice, Elizabeth A. Weaver entitled, *Judicial Deceit: Tyranny and Unnecessary Secrecy at the Michigan Supreme Court* [Elizabeth A. Weaver, David B. Schock] . It is Justice Weaver's assertion that not only is the Michigan Supreme Court and the justice system in Michigan corrupt, but the entire process and system needs a major overhaul. The Supreme Court in Michigan oversees the Judicial Tenure Commission, Attorney Grievance Commission and the State Court Administrator's Office.

According to Weaver, the citizens in Michigan have been put at risk by those in power, and those who have asserted power. Most citizens are either apathetic to what occurs, or are blind to the justice system. We are raised to respect authority. Therefore, people blindly respect our judges and hold them in high regard. What else would one do with someone that has the power to take your freedom?

It is assumed that the robed ones would be worthy of the position. Time and time again, our judiciary is exposed to the corruption within. At one point Justice Weaver asserts, when describing the Michigan Supreme Courts decisions and process "So it's Soviet Union type stuff, rewriting history; it didn't happen." (Page 463, Judicial Deceit).

It was a head scratcher when Lucille Taylor (former Michigan Governor John Engler's judicial appointments officer) appointed her husband to the Michigan Supreme Court. The culture rose to another level when Governor Rick Snyder's judicial appointments officer, Michael Gadola, appointed himself to the Michigan Court of Appeals.

The Finest Judges Money Can Buy, by Charles R. Ashman, and *The Best Judges that Money Can Buy*, by Nancy Perry Graham, are examples of the bad apples within the system. One could study Operation Graylord in Chicago for more examples of corrupt judges. Justic

Weaver, however, points to a systemic problem. Outside sources have consistently ranked Michigan last in the United States. These studies would seem to concur with Justice Weaver's assessment of the mess in Michigan. The Federal Judiciary differs in Michigan in many respects; one being that the judges are appointed for life in the federal system. Life meant something entirely different in the late1700's by our forefathers writing our constitution than what it means today. Both Federal and State judges come from the same culture—society.

***

The morning of trial, before the attorneys went into the courtroom where prospective jurors were seated, the defense attorneys objected to Judge Quist regarding the lapel pins worn by Matt and Col. Odom. Matt was active in Rotary and liked his Rotary President's pin. John was proud of his military service and liked to wear his Air Force Pin. It was a miniature version of the Legion of Merit Medal he received upon his latest retirement. For each it was just a matter of habit and didn't think anything of it. The defense thought it could cause unfair prejudice. While the pins were very small and difficult to discern from a distance, the defense counsel objected to them, and Judge Quist made Matt remove his.

Hurleys' team would roll with the punches. So, there would be no expert witnesses on the SCRA, military orders and the effect of active duty on a servicemember, no punitives, no attorney Voir Dire, and no Rotary pin. The Hurleys had waited since 2004 for their justice, and they were not about to be completely denied. Justice delayed is justice denied, and James would never get his home back. He was never really going to be able to go home. But what would happen when he returned home after this trial would hopefully mean something for everyone in the military.

The team decided to move to Grand Rapids. Since Col. Odom was the senior member of the team, a Colonel, an integral part of the trial strategy, and such a larger than life figure, he received the largest bedroom. Dan drove in from Detroit every day, so he didn't need a room. Frank and Matt purchased single beds and took over the family room. They felt so strongly that the case would settle that Matt refused to unpack during the first week. Hurley's team could not believe that the case would not settle. In the history of the nation, a jury had never heard such a case. How in the world could these defendants risk going to verdict? The defendants should have begged the Hurleys to settle.

The weeks before trial, Col. Odom shared his involvement with the Department of Justice. The DOJ had followed the Hurley case for the past two years and had gathered information about seventy other soldiers that the defendant bank illegally foreclosed upon. With the Hurley case, the DOJ would try for a global settlement. Due to the contact from the DOJ, Hurley trial settlement talks occurred only through Col. Odom and the senior attorney for the bank's trial team. The bank hired a private, large Detroit firm for trial. Surely they would milk the case to the very end.

The motivation for defense attorneys to bill by the hour to simply settle a case does not exist. Their motive was to take a case through trial; billable hours. Settlement talks were simply unproductive; the bank was still suing the Hurleys and wanted money for the deficiency. Unbeknownst to Hurley's team was what the defense was hiding relating to their illegal SCRA policy. The Hurley team felt that once the involvement of the DOJ became known to the defense attorneys, they would have to settle.

Unfortunately, the bank refused to negotiate other than through the senior attorney they were going to use for trial. His clock was running. This all had become bigger than this defense attorney, and the bank needed a self-assessment of what was going on. The case was going to trial. Days before they moved to Grand Rapids, Hurley's team ran the Federal Court's Judicial Disclosures pertaining to Judge Quist. His rulings simply did not make sense and the team wanted to know more information about the judge. According to Quist's financial disclosures, he had several investment accounts with the defendant bank and its parent company.

Aside from (or in addition to) his ultra conservatism, the health of his investments may have had some impact on decisions he made relating to this case. At the very least, in accordance with the judicial code of professional conduct, it simply gave rise to an appearance of impropriety.

The second judge assigned to this case, Judge Maloney in Kalamazoo, Michigan, recused himself from the case for this very same investment reason. Accordingly, plaintiffs filed a motion for Judge Quist to recuse himself from the case. As one would guess, he refused to leave the case. The Hurleys had come too far and seemed to have to battle with this judge more than what the case precedent and the SCRA envisioned or anticipated.

The Hurley team had hired a prominent Grand Rapids attorney to assist with local issues just as they did with Dan in Detroit, as there was always a need for local boots on the ground. Ironically, Judge Quist's magistrate's incredulous comments toward Matt and the hiring of additional attorneys for a team approach, was showing its importance. The magistrate was correct in her assessment that given the SCRA, it should not have been so complicated to prosecute the Hurley case. Hurley was a team effort. The old adage that, "There is no "I" in team," certainly applied. A case of such significance could not rest on egos and personalities.

It took Michael Jordan seven seasons in the NBA before the team won a championship. Bill Billechek had losing seasons in Cleveland before the team he won the championships with in New England. Time and again and in all facets of life, we see that people, as individuals, need help. A team of lawyers needed to work together to save a home; that was illegally foreclosed. It was not a time to be selfish. Matt wanted as many great people as he could get to help the Hurleys.

Frank Melchiore had a friend in Grand Rapids who was willing to help the team. This prominent Grand Rapids attorney withdrew from the case after the Hurleys filed the Motion for recusal. He knew Judge Quist and felt the recusal motion would surely set the jurist off. Essentially, the Hurley attorneys were calling into question Quist's honor.

CHAPTER 20
"YES, WE MADE MISTAKES"

The morning of jury selection was dark and painfully cold. Snow and ice covered the roads. The wind chill brought temperatures well below freezing. Yes Col. Odom, the Magnolias and Azalea's were in full bloom in Shreveport.

From the parking garage to the Federal Plaza, numerous patriotic individuals walked carrying American and military flags. The demonstrators were not saying anything, but obviously they looked like supporters of our armed forces. Some carried handmade signs to show support for Sgt. James Hurley.

The defendants protested to the judge, who was oblivious to the demonstrator's presence. But he scolded the Hurley team anyway, in the event they were some how involved with these Americans who showed support to a U.S. soldier. "Surely Plaintiffs' counsel would not be involved with such behavior," Quist warned.

Weather conditions prohibited the demonstrators from being around too long anyway, and Quist said that it was not unusual to have somebody doing something out on the plaza. Therefore, he dismissed any curative effect the defendants requested he take with the potential jury pool. The demonstrators, heroically and honorably fought the harsh winter weather for the first week. Many came in from the elements and were welcome to observe the proceedings; some even stayed through the duration of the trial.

Their presence was greatly appreciated by Sgt. Hurley, Brandie, Valla, and the entire Hurley team. No one knew where they had come from, but their efforts inspired and kept Sgt. Hurley and his team on task. They were true Americans, and loyalists to the country's soldiers. Many of them were proud and honorable veterans. "Yes, ladies and gentlemen of the jury, we made mistakes," said the slick trial attorney for the law firm defendant who had been hired a month earlier. It was part of his opening statement. It had taken the Hurley family nearly seven years to get their day in court and now Sgt. Hurley was forced to hear a sarcastic and disingenuous opening statement from someone who had just gotten into the case. What did he know?

Flashback to the year 1997.

The judge's opinion started out with two words: "The truth." "What is the truth?" These words came from the historic case of Traxler vs. Ford Motor Company. The case was fascinating for Frank Melchiore and Matt Cooper, mostly because it was in front of their favorite State court judge in Grand Rapids, the Honorable Dennis Kolenda. Judge Kolenda defaulted Ford Motor Company for abuses occurred during discovery—hiding evidence. The deceit became so severe that the company was no longer entitled to participate in the trial. Traxler won by default.

The slick trial counsel hired by Ford for the Traxler case was the very same attorney who appeared in the Hurley trial for the defendant law firm. He tried cases all over the country with his smooth and flashy act. A month prior to the Hurley trial, a jury decided against his Ohio client for millions. He would try to appear apologetic to the jury about the mistakes they made in the Hurley case. He was willing to say or do anything.

Throughout the trial, the defense attorneys would frequently stoop to child-like behavior. Their opening statements were a joke. The jury heard the snide comments from the counsel's table during the witness examinations. During Matt's examination of Hurley's superior officers in Iraq, the ankle biting and childish comments from the bank's attorney was constant throughout the testimony. Matt stood at the podium just in front of the defense table.

The female attorney who had been in charge of the bank's defense from the beginning, made sarcastic sounds from the defense table; just soft enough not to be heard by the court or jury. She couldn't keep her mouth shut. Her husband was an army officer, so of course she knew more than the rest of us...she had been telling us that for years. She did not have any direct trial involvement with the case, so her condescending whimpering was all she could have. It was amusing so let her have it.

A tactic not acceptable was the bank's lead trial attorney who acted as though he had fallen asleep. At some point during the trial he actually would dose off. Finally, Judge Quist did something for the Hurleys... or did he? On more than one occasion, he called all of the attorneys to the bench and told the bank's lawyer not to fall asleep in front of the jury. It is very disrespectful and it could hurt his client.

The first week of trial came to a close. The case was starting to move along at a snail's pace due to the plaintiffs' need (as set by the judge) to establish proofs sufficient for an award of punitive damages. He had long ago ruled that punitive damages were out. Politically, tort reform simply did not have any consideration of punitive damages. Matt felt that conservatism must have been a driving force within Judge Quist that caused him to make the plaintiffs go above and beyond what the SCRA required for a punitive assessment.

Plain and simple, the SCRA allows for punitive damages. However, Judge Quist required the Hurleys to put forth evidence that would justify an award. They had to prove the case as if the bank sought a judicial action originally. Essentially, Hurley had to submit proofs sufficient for the judge to warrant a punitive award. This uphill battle was created by Judge Quist, and was not something the SCRA required.

The judge had already ruled the foreclosure was illegal, yet he also determined that the eviction was not, and the Hurleys could not asse_ otherwise to the jury. Judge Quist had boxed the Hurleys in. As_ from what Valla went through, Judge Clarke stated that when he entered a default against Sergeant Hurley on June 14, 2005:

"[A]t no time during the eviction proceedings do I recall being informed that an individual was present in the courthouse on behalf of James Hurley and claiming to be an occupant of the house...As a result that neither Sergeant Hurley nor any other occupants of the house came forward to express their questions and/or concerns, I signed a Default Judgment, which contained the provision that "for a defendant on active military duty, default judgment shall not be entered except as provided by [the SCRA].""

Not only did the defendants pull the wool over Judge Clarke's eyes, they then improperly used the order he signed, which expressly limited its use to be in compliance with the SCRA. The Odomism of "let them go to Congress and change it if they do not like it", was the basis for Col. Odom's draft of changes to the SCRA as a result of the judicial activism with a conservative slant taken by Judge Quist. A U.S. soldier does not need to be taken to task under the SCRA, as was what was happening in the conservative banking enclave of West Michigan. This literally was the second time Col. Odom had visited Michigan for Hurley, and he was beginning to hope to never step foot in the state again.

The team worked for days to put forth Valla's testimony. She was adamant that she made all of the mortgage payments while her son was in Iraq. Maybe she was late on one, but all of the payments were made. She testified that she thought that James had such a great ten-year history on the mortgage, that a late payment would not be a problem. Valla stood her ground about the evidence that she and the guard units faxed to the mortgage servicing company in Texas. Time and time again, the defendants spent hour after hour in an effort to impeach everything that Valla testified to.

They tried to discredit her attempt to verify the payment history, the notice of active duty and the cleaning out of the house. They refused to believe that she did not want to live in the cottage, or that she did nothing to stop the eviction. They discredited her character, work history, and motives in her care for the mentally challenged. The defendants patronized Valla to the jury as the mastermind behind the loss of the home. They said she wanted him to get rid of the river home, and was happy it was gone. After days of being grilled by the defendants, Valla began to feel maybe it was all her fault.

She left the courtroom and embraced Lisa, Matt's assistant in the hall-way. For as solid and firm as Valla appeared on the witness stand, Lisa could just feel the intense trembling and shaking throughout her body as Valla grabbed her hand. In tears, Valla explained to Lisa that she clearly remembered sending all of those documents and making the payments. How could these defendants make her out to be such a liar?

The defendants were playing the judge's hand. Yes, there were mis-takes made, but simply mistakes; nothing that would rise to the level to justify punitive damages. While the Hurleys were wronged, it was really no one's fault. Just the fact his home was taken, in violation of the SCRA while he was on active duty, did not justify a financial award. The court's decision was contrary to law. The Hurley's loss was immeasurable, painful. The SCRA states that they are entitled to punitive damages.

Beyond these arguments, the Hurley team set forth a clear need for the assessment of punitive damages. It was not just a simple mistake. The defendants had a clear policy that required servicemembers to provide their individual orders for SCRA protections. The policy, in and of itself, violated the SCRA. Punitive damages were necessary to stop such a policy. The Hurley trial was supposed to be on damages only. They were to prove what type of damages the Hurleys sustained. What should be available to them became next to impossible because of what Judge Quist required, and what evidence from the defendants, the plaintiffs possessed.

Unlike on television and in the movies, there should not be any sur-prises at trial. In Federal Court in particular, the discovery rules are open and clear. There is no wiggle room for hide-the-ball type tactics. Federal Court disclosure rules require everything to be disclosed. Even things that may have an ever so slight, remote connection to a case must be turned over to the opposing party.

The Hurley trial team needed to establish that Judge Quist ruled the foreclosure illegal as a matter of law. It was known that the affidavit signed by the foreclosing law office was false. So what? The sworn document declared the opposite of Sgt. Hurley's military status. It was all just a simple mistake, an innocent mistake. They do thousands of foreclosures a week in all eighty-three Michigan counties. How could they possibly be burdened to actually check the truth and veracity of each and every one of the tens, hundreds, thousands of affidavits they sign?

Even though Col. Odom displayed how it takes seconds to discern active duty status on the Department of Defense website, the defense felt they could not be expected to be burdened in such a manner. They claimed, it was just a simple innocent mistake that Sgt. Hurley slipped through the cracks. No one knew this was happening. No one wanted it to happen. The primary attorney for the foreclosure mill that signed court papers, testified in his deposition that he would simply take the stack of papers out of a basket and sign his name to them. He never read them. He did not review them. He would simply sign where necessary and execute all of the documents that were in his to-be-signed basket.

In his deposition, it was obvious that he was ashamed of his behavior and that he was simply trying to perform the job tasks that were assigned. Matt's heart went out to him because he seemed to be a person that had achieved educational success, and he knew that this was not the position that he dreamt of when he had aspired to become an attorney. He just came to work, and signed where he was told. He did not have his own office.

He worked in a building where he had never been to other floors, and didn't know where things were located. The entire building housed the foreclosure mill law office. Hundreds of employees were restricted to their designated areas. Once a week, a semi truck and trailer-size paper shredder came to the building to purge documents.

Why (if the defense were to be believed) should they pay Hurley for the deficiency and what he put them through during the last five years of litigation? Of course they weren't going to push the jury that far, but they were getting close. The case was knee deep in a quagmire of horse and cow shit. Frank Melchiore had the pleasure of calling the defendant law firm's senior vice president and litigation specialist to the witness stand. She just so happened to be the wife of the defendant law firm's initial attorney–the hand puppeteer.

Mrs. Senior VP took the witness stand and almost immediately gave new meaning to the phrase crying "crocodile tears". Frank is an expert in conducting witness examinations. He is smooth, calm, and most importantly, precise on the question and answer that he expects. The rule, "never ask a question you do not know the answer to" was taken to new heights under Frank's examination. His precision in his answer expectation is focused on anticipation of a deviation from the response he expects.

A deviation by the witness—especially a hostile witness or one that thinks she is directing the tone and direction of the examination—falls prey to Frank's simple exposure of the truth. Federal courts swear witnesses to tell the truth. The expression of "the truth shall set you free" could not have a better example than with Mrs. Senior VP's experience in the Hurley case.

The morning she took the stand seemed like any other day of the trial. The Hurleys and their trial team did not have any feeling or expectation that anything extraordinary was going to happen that day. It was expected that she was going to try and come across as sympathetic. She appeared as a warm and loving person, a young mother that was kind and considerate. She, just like everyone else, felt horrible about what happened to the Hurleys. While completely innocent, she felt really bad that mistakes happened and she bawled like a little baby to prove it.

Breaks had to be taken to allow her to gain her composure. She made Frank walk a fine line of appearing to beat up on her to obtain sympathy from the jury. Clearly her tactic was to show that she had done no wrong. Why was Frank humiliating her in front of the jury? After all, she felt sorry for the Hurleys. Mrs. Senior VP's goals, objectives, and strategy for her testimony, coupled with Frank's calm precision of anticipation, led to an explosion. Lawyers have to be able to think on their feet. This means that when there are deviations from the demands of precise expectations, there has to be acceptance and changes, and movements in the examiner's line of questioning. The slight subtle deviations lead to the biggest treasure troves of information.

When Mrs. Senior VP provided answers, it became increasingly apparent that she was referencing and relying upon documents the Hurley team was not aware of and had never seen. She referenced a whole communication network between the defendant law firm and the defendant mortgage-servicing representatives in Texas. An email system contained years of communication and the exchange of documents.

Thus far, there had been days and days of testimony in an attempt to show the jury information that the Hurley team tried to prove actually existed. Mrs. Senior VP's testimony proved in fact, that this information did in fact exist and the defendants were aware of it and possessed it the whole time. The communications should have been turned over years ago; during the depositions of the law firm defendant employees and the initial disclosures.

The Texas depositions, which should have taken one or maybe two days, required months to complete. Typically whenever Dan and Frank got a witness to disclose not just factual issues, but the existence of documents that reflected the knowledge of Sgt. Hurley's active duty status, the bank's attorney would object and declare that all of the documents relating to the subject matter were provided.

The bank's attorney's declaration would prompt Dan and Frank to inquire into the veracity of the defendant's testimony concerning the existence of other documents upon which the deponent (an employee of the mortgage-servicing company in Texas who had nothing to hide or a desire to act in an illegal fashion) would disclose the existence of further documents. The deposition would then come to a halt so that the deponent could go into the mortgage servicer's records and search for the documents they referenced in their deposition.

Under the federal court rules, all of the documents the mortgage serving company had in its possession relating to Sgt. Hurley, should have been turned over years earlier. The notice for the deponents' depositions required the turning over of any documents that related to the Hurley case prior to their deposition testimony. There were no documents provided by the mortgage- servicing company to the Hurleys or their attorneys.

But for the questions posed by Dan and Frank, the existence of any documents would not have been known. This is in complete contradiction of the Federal Court rules. The defendants were in violation of the disclosure requirements. Not only did the defendants attempt to "hide the ball", they were engaged in conduct that even denied the existence of a ball.

The bank's attorney continued to declare that upon the discovery of a new document that "this is it, there are no more documents." Further questioning of the deponent would reveal the existence of more documents. The incredible obvious hiding of materials necessitated the filing of Motions to Compel with the court, given that the interruption by the bank's attorney during the depositions were causing ineffective discovery. It was clear that the attorney had guided employees of the mortgage-servicing department in Texas not to provide the documents that in fact did exist.

Frank's interrogation of Mrs. Senior VP cracked the vault. The mortgage-servicing company in fact, had all of the Active Duty Orders that Valla had sent to them. Further, there were email communications between the mortgage servicing company and the foreclosure attorneys, which discussed the active duty status, and the ramifications of his active duty with the legality of the process they were undertaking

under the non-judicial foreclosure. The mortgage servicing department also had extensive documented communications between the
Hurley family and mortgage servicing representatives concerning the
missing of payments and Sgt. Hurley's active duty status, as well as
Sgt. Hurley's active duty status of being stationed in Iraq. Clearly, the
mortgage-servicing department had documented evidence that related
to the Hurley family concerning the non-judicial foreclosure and the
eviction proceedings.

Unfortunately, at the time of the depositions, and as a result of the Motion to Compel, none of the documents were turned over or produced
for the Hurleys or their attorneys. The very existence of this evidence
would not have been known to the Hurley attorneys had it not been
for Mrs. Senior VP's break down on the witness stand. On numerous
occasions, she broke down bawling because she had such a struggle
disclosing the documents that had been hidden from the Hurleys.

Specifically, she struggled with her requirement and desire to tell the
truth with the defendants' defense strategy that this had all been a ter-
rible mistake. The documents disclosed that the foreclosure itself was
anything but a mistake, and the defendants' defense tactics were clearly an effort to hide the intentional violation of the laws concerning the
foreclosure and active duty military personnel. She clearly was in a
quandary that could only allow her to be set free upon telling the truth.
She, single-handedly blew the lid off the defendants' conduct during
the illegal foreclosure and the past five years of the case.

At the time of Valla's grilling by the defendants, the posture of the
case at that time was that plaintiffs tried to prove events that were
explained away as mistakes by the defense. The defendants directly
challenged Valla and her testimony about James' payments. They
challenged whether she had actually notified anyone of his active duty
status. None of it was claimed by the defense as being deliberately
ignored. There was never any proactive action, just innocent mistakes
and reactions that resulted in a horrible occurrence.

Valla was put through such a grueling test she was not only beginning to question herself as to what she remembered, but was also beginning to question her own sanity. All of this was to be set upside down by Mrs. Senior VP's testimony. Everything they had questioned Valla on and called into dispute, they knew was true and accurate. By afternoon, after many delays due to Mrs. Senior VP's bouts of crying, documents were revealed and brought to light for the Hurley team for the first time. These documents made most of what the plaintiffs put the jury through a complete waste of time. The plaintiffs feared that the jury would be turned off by what appeared to be a confusing submission of evidence by the plaintiffs. The defendants' strategy of confusion was again playing into their hands.

Generally, jurors honorably sit through jury duty. They are willing to do their civic duty; sometimes at great cost to their employment pay and family responsibilities. All they ask in return is that the lawyers and court do not waste their time. Lawyers who try to garner their attention in their favor certainly do not want to be blamed for making them sit through a week and a half of trial. By all appearances, it seemed (based on the documents and communications shared by Mrs. Senior VP) that defendants knew information that completely contradicted every position they had taken or asserted. The jury would not understand the discovery violations. They would only blame the plaintiffs for wasting the week.

Sometime after the trial resolution, some of the trial defense attorneys even disclosed their surprise and astonishment to the plaintiffs attorneys when it became obvious to them that there was no way the plaintiffs attorney understood the treasure trove of information contained in these emails and communications. Yet oddly, but not surprisingly, given these defense attorneys, they tried to capitalize on the misinformation.

After all the humiliation they put Valla through, all of what she claimed was there in black and white. The information that supported Valla's answers was discovered and the defense knew it. Communications between the law firm and the mortgage servicing company established their knowledge of Sgt. Hurley's active duty status and the decisio to keep forging forward. Discussions about the faxed documents that Valla personally sent from the corner gas station. They had called her a liar about this, stating she couldn't possibly remember sending the fax. But she did. And there was information–backing up Valla and showing that they knew, contrary to their attempts to impeach her. Communication entries summarized phone calls made by Valla to challenge the paper history back in 2004, and entries about Valla and Brandie's call about James being in Iraq and on active duty were there as well.

Message entries summarized a call from the Cash for Keys realtor, which notified them of his concern about James being gone in Iraq. There also was special mention by the eviction attorney about the process server's hand-written note about James being on active duty in Iraq. Direct communications among the defendants showed discussion that verified the Department of Defense website search that found Sgt. Hurley was on active duty at the time of the foreclosure.

Entries showed discussions of the defendants at the most critical stage of the illegal foreclosure; at the time the redemption period would have run, but for Sgt. Hurley's active duty status. One (as with many of the other communications) contained writings and opinions from Mrs. Senior VP herself. The correspondence discussed the SCRA and Sgt. Hurley's active duty status. There was proof that the decision was made to continue forward despite his active duty status and their knowledge that they were violating the SCRA.

Amazingly, Valla's memory of all of this was like a steel trap. Everything she said was received and known by these defendants, yet they cross-examined her on all of the details as if she were lying and confused. There was written proof that they were aware of the fraud perpetrated to obtain the wrongful eviction, that Judge Quist deemed legal, and something that the Hurley team could not call into question.

Innocent? No. Mistakes? No. They felt bad? No. Could not have been avoided? No. Complied with the SCRA? No. Absent of mal-'ce with intent? No. There is no possible or conceivable legitimate excuse for the defendants to have kept this information from the Hurleys. Years of deception by these defendants were just exposed in documents that had been hidden from the plaintiffs. Just as they knowingly violated the SCRA, they knowingly attempted to hide and lie their way through the litigation of the case.

The system's goal to find the truth had been violated. All of the reasons behind Judge Kolenda's rulings in Traxler vs. Ford Motor Company had just been laid out on this day in the Hurley Trial. The defendants' conduct in the Hurley case led to an illegal foreclosure and numerous violations of the Hurley family rights under the SCRA. The court's failure to timely resolve the case and allow the defendants to run and hide, only served to postpone and cement their position and tactics to do wrong.

There really was not an internal SCRA policy that required a servicemember to provide their independent order to obtain mortgage foreclosure relief. While there is an SCRA requirement for such a provision for the interest rate reduction, the bank and mortgage company had no such technical requirement. Mrs. Senior VP's document entries proved that. They knew, and had discussions that any such SCRA internal policy did not exist; it was merely a legal fiction, a lie, fabricated as a defense tactic of the bank's attorneys. Yes, there was an SCRA policy of the defendants that violated the SCRA, that was simply to say, "To hell with active duty and the SCRA." Their SCRA policy was not to follow the SCRA on foreclosures.

Obviously, when you have a soldier sending in a form their unit gave them to send in declaring the SCRA requirements and the specific requests that they be granted an interest rate reduction provides notice of active duty. The defendants had shown malice, intent, and a complete act of fraud and deception. The elements necessary to prove a case for punitive damages could not have been more clear.

It was an intentional act of fraud and deceit by the defendants' attorneys on the court and to the jury. It was a made up Mea Culpa in an attempt to avoid punitive damages. The original acts were fraudulen and illegal when committed, and now the trial counsel had committed equally illegal acts to cover them up and try to portray them as simple mistakes. The false affidavit was a mistake. They did not know how to check on active duty status? Bull roar – they knew James was on active duty and there were documents that clearly set that knowledge out and the documents were hidden throughout the years of litigation and the efforts to keep them hidden continued through trial.

For the law firm that was sued, it was an easy practice of deception. Up until trial, their lawsuit attorneys were in-house attorneys. Their lies and illegal acts were kept secret. When they needed litigation attorneys, it was ironic that it was the Ford attorney from the Traxler case.

Regarding the bank and the mortgage servicing company, it became clear why the lead attorney went through five law firms before the final trial counsel was chosen. As much as some in society find it easy to lawyer bash, it is refreshing to see how difficult it was for her to find a group of attorneys willing to perpetrate her fraud and illegal acts. How ironic that her lead trial counsel was the same one who worked to keep the owner of a bridge in Detroit out of prison.

They counter-sued the Hurleys and submitted frivolous offers of judgment, all the while knowing they engaged in illegal activity. Illegal activity to hide illegal activity. Their Motions to Dismiss and for Summary Judgment were based on fraud. They hid evidence up to, and during trial that illegal acts were committed to effectuate the foreclosure and sale in violation of the SCRA. The litigation tactics throughout the past years, and the chosen trial tactics of covering up the illegal acts, constituted the illegal acts to cover up the illegal acts.

This is why lead counsel for the bank bounced the case from three to five different law firms. Theories were discussed as to why the mega-firms and their specialty trial teams would come and go. Ultimately, it was realized that when the mega-firms' attorneys learned how the bank's lead attorney hid evidence and tried to cover up illegal policies and practices, the hired guns quietly withdrew. They would easily be replaced by another big firm that was willing to rev up their billing machine for one of the world's largest banks. The withdrawing firms and its attorneys chose loyalty to the client over duty to the tribunal and system. Ironically, it was later learned by Hurley's team, that the eventual head of the bank's trial team was the FBI character reference for Judge Quist when the judge was cleared for his appointment to the bench by President Bush twenty years earlier. The whole thing just stunk; from the illegal foreclosure, to the morning of the filing of the Motion for Default.

The next morning, the Hurley attorneys filed a Motion for Default or in the alternative, a Mistrial. After filing the motion, defense counsel scrambled in an effort to control the damage their witness had caused the previous day. After several hours of discussion amongst counsel and the court, it was determined that the trial would not continue for that day. The jury was sent home.

Given the proofs in place it is important to examine Judge Quist's opinions about damages in the light of what was shown.

Judge Quist in Hurley, 08-cv-361, 2009 WL 701006 (W.D. Mich. March 13, 2009) stated that the SCRA does not intend to limit the type of damages available to those who have been aggrieved by violations. It would be ridiculous and vituperative to ever limit claims, for instance, to just breach of contract-type damages.

Congress must have intended to provide a means of enforcing the special rights it created in favor of servicemembers, otherwise, rights granted by the SCRA would essentially be illusory. In addition, the right conferred upon servicemembers under § 533(c) – to have a mortgagee foreclose a mortgage only through a court action– is a right not available to the public at large.

Finally, the rights granted under§ 533 are very similar to those at issue in Marin and Linscott under § 531 and §537, respectively. The Court reaches the same conclusion with regard to §526, which excludes a period of military service from any period of redemption of real property. The right or benefit granted under this section is al not available to the public, and a servicemember would be unable to obtain relief for a violation of this provision absent an implied right of action.

Regarding § 531, requiring a court order to evict, the Court concludes that a private right of action also exists for violations of this section. While it is true that in Michigan self-help is prohibited and landlords are required to resort to eviction proceedings under the summary proceedings act, see Mier v. Zimmerman, No. 273312, 2008 WL 681158, at *3 (Mich. Ct. App. Mar.13, 2008), § 531(b) grants servicemembers a right to obtain a stay of execution during a period of military service under certain circumstances. This right is unavailable to ordinary citizens.

In his opinion dated February 4, 2011, Judge Quist addressed the issue of damages under the SCRA as follows:

A.   Damages Under the SCRA Because the SCRA is a federal statute designed to promote the military defense of the United States, the Court finds that it should look [to] federal law to determine the appropriate measure of damages for a violation of the Act, including whether non-economic damages are available. It would not make much sense to have state-by-state adjudications regarding national defense. Where, as here, the Court has recognized an implied right of action under a federal statute, it must "presume the availability of all appropriate remedies unless Congress has expressly indicated otherwise." Franklin Gwinnett Cnty Pub. Schs, 503 U.S. 60, 66, 112 S. Ct. 1028, 1031 (1992).

The parties have presented no case law, and legal research revealed none, discussing what types of damages are appropriate in an action under the SCRA. Although Defendants urge the Court to limit Plaintiffs' damages to those available for breach of contract, the Court finds that an action under the SCRA is more analogous to an action under consumer-protection-type statutes, such as the Fair Debt Collection Practices Act ("FDCPA"), 15 U.S.C. §§1692 et seq., or the Fair Credit Reporting Act ("FCRA"), 15 U.S.C. § 1681 et seq., than it is to a breach of contract.

The FDCPA and the FCRA provide various procedural protections and rights to a defined class of persons – consumers. Similarly the SCRA provides procedural protections and rights to a defined class of persons. Moreover, violations of federal rights give rise to tort-like claims. See e.g., 42 U.S.C. § 1983.

Under both the FDCPA and the FCRA, "non-economic damages" are recoverable as a component of actual damages, including damages for personal humiliation, embarrassment, mental anguish and/or emotional distress. See Bach v First Union Nat. Bank, 149 F. App'x 354, 3651 (6th Cir. 2005); Hoffman v GC Servs. Ltd. P'ship, et al., No. 3:08-cv-255, (E.D. Teen. May 11, 2010) (citing Milton v Rosicki, Rosicki & Assoc., P.C., 2007 WL 226893, at *3 (E.D.N.Y. 2007); Pourfard v Equifax Info. Co., 45 F. 3d 129, 1333 (9th Cir. 1995).

Accordingly, the Court holds that non-economic damages, including mental anguish and emotional distress, are also recoverable for a violation of the SCRA. Moreover, to prove such damages, Plaintiffs need not meet the same standards required by Michigan law to establish intentional or negligent infliction of emotional distress. See Hoffman, supra, at *29-31 (noting a split in authority on the issue, but holding that emotional damages may be recovered under the FDCPA without proving the elements of state law claims for intentional or negligent infliction of emotional distress).

In fact, Plaintiffs' own testimony may suffice, so long as it sufficiently explains the injury and consists of more than merely conclusory statements. See Bach, 149 F. App.'x at 361.

Quist further stated in his Opinion of March 13, 2009:

The final issue is whether punitive damages are allowed under the SCRA. Predictably, Defendants cite Michigan law, which does not allow for punitive damages. Plaintiffs, on the other hand, contend that Texas law should control, apparently because that is where Deutsche Bank's headquarters are located. The Court need not choose between the two, because both parties are wrong. The SCRA is a federal law, and therefore, federal law should control the determination of the issue. (Emphasis added).

Where a private right of action is judicially implied, the court has "a measure of latitude to shape a sensible remedial scheme that best comports with the statute." Gebser v Lago Vista Indep. Sch. Dist., 524 U.S. 274, 284, 118 S. Ct. 1989, 1996 (1998). Determining a proper remedy "inherently entails a degree of speculation, since it addresses an issue on which Congress has not specifically spoken." Id.

The statute at issue should guide the issue, to ensure that the remedy is not at odds with the statutory structure and purpose. Id. The Court thus begins with the statute. According to § 502, the purposes of the SCRA are:

(1) to provide for, strengthen, and expedite the national defense through protection extended by [the SCRA] to servicemembers of the United States to enable such persons to devote their energy to the defense needs of the Nation; and

(2) to provide for the temporary suspension of judicial and administrative proceedings and transactions that may adversely affect the civil rights of servicemembers during their military service.

50 U.S.C. App. § 502. While the SCRA is to be construed liberally in favor of servicemembers, "it is not to be used as a sword against persons with legitimate claims. Engstrom v First Nat'l Bank of Eagle Lake, 47 F. 3d 1459, 462 (5th Cir.1995).

Apart from the stated purpose of the act, Congress included provisions concerning preservation of other remedies in various sections of the SCRA providing specific rights to servicemembers. For example, §533(d)(2) provides:

(2) Preservation of other remedies. The remedies and rights provided under this section are in addition to and do not preclude any remedy for wrongful conversion otherwise available under law to the person

claiming relief under this section, including consequential and punitive damages.

50 U.S.C. App. §533(d)(2). As noted above, the court in Linscott concluded that a similar provision under § 537(c) indicated that Congress did not intend to deny the remedy of damages to servicemembers. Linscott, 2006 WL 240529, at *7.

While the question is not free from doubt, this Court concludes that punitive damages may be recovered for SCRA violations. In Franklin v Gwinnett County Public Schools, 503 U.S. 60, 112 S. Ct. 1028 (1992), the Supreme Court said that in implying a right of action, "we presume the availability of all appropriate remedies unless Congress has expressly indicated otherwise." Id. At 66, 112 S. Ct. At 1033. Because there is no indication in the statute that Congress intended to exclude punitive damages as a remedy, the Court finds no basis to conclude that such damages are unavailable. Hurley v Deutsche Bank, et al., No. 08-cv-361, 2009 WL 701006 (W.D. Mich. March 13, 2009).

In waiting to find out the next course of action, the Hurley Team went to lunch. For the most part, the attorneys didn't care where they ate, however, Col. Odom had one requirement – the establishment must have cloth napkins. Thus, the attorneys found themselves at an establishment that they had been to numerous times throughout the trial. After they were seated by the hostess and eased into conversation about the previous day's testimony, Col. Odom discovered that the menu–the same menu he had looked at on numerous occasions—was doubled-sided.

The conversation briefly ensued concerning the newly discovered menu options. The health conscious Italians asked if the soup of the day was cream or broth-based? Could they substitute salad for the fries? Could the chef hold the bacon and cheese from their grilled sandwiches? Colonel Odom and Matt decided on steaks from the newly discovered second page. At the same time, they volunteered to eat the bacon and cheese from Frank and Dan's sandwiches, and don't forget the chef's special, Roasted Duck, that Odom and Matt ordered to share. Yes, while the Italians were health conscious and physically fit, Matt could always put up more on the bench and triple their best on the dip rack.

CHAPTER 21

THERE IS JUSTICE IN AMERICA

*T*he *Malaysian Sun* had its fun poking at America, but there is justice in America. As much as the United States of America is the land of opportunity, it does have a system that sometimes allows justice to prevail. It does mandate and require fights, fortitude, and unwavering commitment, but it is a system where even David can overcome Goliath.

The SCRA violations by the defendants were done on purpose and were intentional. The defendants' asserted defenses by their attorneys that were known to be frivolous and legal fictions, completely contrary to the facts, as they knew them to have occurred and hid from the Hurleys and their attorneys. Hurley's case evolved because the defendants were much too busy to concern themselves with the SCRA. Part of the defendant's illegal business model depended upon the strength and durability of the U.S. soldier. The men and women in our military are strong warriors that when they are knocked down, they pull themselves up by the bootstraps and continue forward.

During the housing collapse that occurred around the Hurley case, many foreclosed homes were under water. The defendant's figured most soldiers were probably upside down on their mortgage. This was the era of robo-signing. Affidavits were false. There was no time to actually have someone sign affidavits. In the Hurley case, the affidavits sworn to be true and accurate were not understood, let alone read by its signator. There was simply not enough time. A law firm with a few hundred employees, focused primarily on foreclosures and collections kept them very busy.

The hidden emails evidenced a clear understanding between the foreclosure law firm and the servicing company. Both shared a desire to forge forward regardless of SCRA requirements. Mrs. Senior VP tried to stay the course with the defendants' legal fiction defenses, however she was boxed in by Frank and was forced to disclose the truth. The Defendants committed one illegal act after another.

The Hurleys were a typical American family that lived paycheck to paycheck. When James was called to California, he went a month without a paycheck. As he purchased the supplies and tools he would need to take to Iraq, a mortgage payment was missed. It was paid quite late. During the mortgage foreclosure crisis of this period, a late payment to the bank was a missed payment. A missed payment triggered foreclosure. While the Hurleys attempted to make good on their debt and provide all of the materials necessary for the Servicemembers' Civil Relief Act to provide its protections to the family, these documents were clearly ignored

Judge Quist made it perfectly clear that he would not entertain a position by the plaintiffs that the eviction of the Hurley family by Judge Clarke in the District Court in South Haven was illegal. The judge felt, and expressed himself quite clearly, that he empathetically would not review the State Court decision in accordance with the Rooker-Feldman Doctrine. The Rooker-Feldman Doctrine is a combination of two United States Supreme Court Opinions that has set forth a basic rule in civil procedure. Rooker v Fidelity Trust Company, 263 U.S. 413 (1923) and District of Columbia Court of Appeals v Feldman, 460 U.S. 462 (1983).

The Rooker-Feldman Doctrine holds that lower United States Federal Courts, being all Federal Courts other than the Supreme Court, should not sit in direct review of State Court decisions unless Congress has specifically authorized such relief. Essentially, it is a ruling that declares that Federal Courts shall not provide a review of what a State

Court has determined. Federal Courts below the Supreme Court shall not become a Court of Appeals for State Court decisions.

The Doctrine has had many different challenges, which seek to define exactly what it means. It has been held to apply to any state court decisions that are judicial in nature. In 2005, the Supreme Court revisited the Doctrine in Exxon Mobil vs. Saudi Basic Industries Corp., 544 U.S. 280. The Court affirmed that the Rooker-Feldman Doctrine was statutory and constitutional. They held that it applied in cases "brought by state court losers complaining of injuries caused by state court judgments rendered before the district court proceedings commenced and inviting district court review and rejection of those judgments." The key words being "seeking court *review* and *rejection* of those judgments."

The Hurleys were not in district court to ask Judge Quist to review and reject the judgments of Judge Clarke. The Hurleys did not seek an appeal of the eviction. The Hurleys did not ask that the eviction judgment be revisited, reviewed, nor rejected. Even the hidden documents expressly stated the defendants' understanding of their illegal conduct in front of Judge Clarke.

The defendants conducted themselves illegally and committed fraud against the trial court and the Hurleys. Judge Quist was ironclad in his determination not to involve the eviction, except to the extent the defendants could state that they behaved in a legal manner. It was an obvious concern of the Hurley attorneys that by allowing the eviction to appear as legal, it would have the effect of counter-acting the claims that the non-judicial foreclosure was not. Essentially, it was feared that a juror would feel that the eviction gave a stamp of approval to the foreclosure.

The non-judicial foreclosure was illegal and allowed the running of a redemption period that never commenced. The sale of the property to a third party, after failing to toll the redemption period was, just as illegal as the fraudulent acts that were perpetrated against Clarke's Court during the eviction proceeding. Judge Quist clearly misapplied

Rooker-Feldman. Given the defendant's brazen ability for illegal acts, and the judge's continuous requirement of an uphill battle, it is surprising to know how well the Hurleys were able to prevail.

It is very unfortunate that the bank was probably not getting the best advice for the money that they spent on legal fees. It seems that the attorneys representing the bank were more concerned about running up their bill and litigating the matter, than in providing the bank with necessary information that concerned their business practices related to the SCRA and soldiers' loans. If only the banks would follow the SCRA, they would receive every penny due to them, just as Lincoln and the drafters of the latest Act envisioned. It could be a win-win for both sides if the protections that are afforded are followed.

Judge Quist would not rule on the Motion for Default or in the Alternative for a Mistrial. It was time for the Hurleys to embrace the situation. Their ordeal was over. The case would end in a settlement of terms, which are the subject of one of the most strict confidential settlement terms any of the involved attorneys had ever been involved. None of the terms may be disclosed. Colonel Odom was quoted in the *New York Times* about the settlement: "The Hurley family is well pleased."

The Hurley case opened the floodgates. During the finalization of the Hurley case settlement terms, while it could not be made a condition, the bank's trial attorney attempted a back slapping, good ole' boy technique of prodding Hurley's attorneys not to file bar grievances with the Attorney Grievance Commission. "Oh, come on boys. He is a good kid," is what he said in referencing the illegal and immoral conduct of the defendant law firm's first attorney. "She just didn't understand," they said, referencing his co-counsel for the bank.

The banks and its attorneys were able to accomplish what they wanted so easily because they were involved in a system conducive to allow fraud and corruption. Even though there was a federal act that protected the Hurleys against exactly what the banks and its attorneys perpetrated against them, the protections were easily circumvented.

The SCRA shield is unable to protect unless there is compliance. The sword created by the Hurley case is unable to penetrate if the judges and the judicial system are not willing, or are incompetent and unable to do their jobs.

The Hurley case portrays the inefficiencies and inadequacies of both the state and federal systems. The judicial environment in Michigan is conducive to the tactics taken. Other than the stumbling blocks inherent within the federal system, the Michigan judiciary failed the Hurleys–not Judge Clarke; the judicial system in Michigan.

Sgt. Hurley no longer gets to enjoy his majestic paradise. He never learned what happened to his 62' Chevy. Most of his clothes and all of his collectibles were gone. Brandie and the girls now live in Texas. And while he is a service-disabled veteran, James counts his blessings daily, and is grateful he returned from the war alive. His greatest reward and vindication was to disclose what the mortgage foreclosure crisis meant to the U.S. Soldier…Lincoln's 21st Century Soldier.

Shortly after the Hurley settlement, a civil class action lawsuit on behalf of servicemembers moved forward in South Carolina, and the United States Department of Justice settled with the defendant bank on behalf of seventy other soldiers that they had illegally foreclosed on. Because of Hurley, and Colonel John S. Odom, Jr., Congress amended the Act that protects all servicemembers. The amendments are referred to as the "Hurley Amendments."

Col. Odom went to Congress because of Judge Quist's rulings and the defense tactics in Hurley and sought amendments. One hopes that there never again will be a judge so confused by the defense tactics. Judge Quist was trying to do the right thing despite his conservatism. It was a struggle. It is ironic that Wikipedia lists Judge Quist's most important case as Hurley…a case that he initially threw out of court.

The SCRA clearly declares that it provides Servicemembers and "any person aggrieved by a violation of this Act" (SCRA Section 597a), a private cause of action. No longer is case law needed to rely upon this and the ability to use the Act as a sword. Further, it provides the servicemember the opportunity to have their attorney fees paid by the Defendants in accordance with the Act. This is a tremendous benefit for servicemembers in that it allows them the opportunity to hire counsel and bring claims for violations.

Never again would a soldier's time be wasted with the frivolous defenses the Hurley defendants raised, or the arguments Judge Quist bought. Six months went by as the Hurleys sat on their hands while Judge Quist's reversed his own ruling. Not only have the U.S. Courts declared that the SCRA provides for a private cause of action, but the Hurley Amendments now state that in plain language so it will never be misunderstood again. Everything that Judge Quist misapplied or misunderstood, his ultra conservative analysis set the foundation for the clarification of the Hurley Amendments (i.e., private right of action and punitive damages are clearly available).

In combating Lincoln's 21st Century Soldiers, financial institutions and the defendants in the Hurley case worked in earnest to discredit the honor and integrity of the soldier and their family. They truly believe the non-judicial foreclosure, the illegal action in taking a soldier's home was a favor to the soldier. They believed that the taking delivered the soldier out from a bad situation. They feel they are better off than they were before the illegal act—never mind that a false affidavit was signed, that a sworn statement made under oath was false, that a perjury occurred. The Soldier is now better off goes the condescending attitude towards our servicemembers.

Many United States Military personnel are preyed upon by unscrupulous lenders who look for a quick return in the form of late fees and a higher interest rate. Hence the SCRA protections relating to a ceiling of a 6% interest rate. The same predatory lender has an attitude that calls for the illegal foreclosure and false affidavits. Just move on, do what is necessary to foreclose and get the soldier and their family out because most of the soldiers will just move on. The few that want to fight and stand up for their rights; for their home, will go down because of who and what they are and an inability to show damages.

That is why Hurley and the Department of Justice actions that followed it were so important. Soldiers' rights are more important than some foreclosure mill's train staying on the tracks and running on time. Soldiers' rights are not merely bumps in the road for these lenders. The United States of America will never overlook the rights of its servicemembers.

Two years after the trial, Hurley was again in the *New York Times* as the paper reported about 200 more soldiers who were illegally foreclosed upon. Department of Justice Director, Tom Perez referred to Hurley when he sought bipartisan support for his appointment by President Obama to the Secretary of Labor position. Hurley laid the groundwork for the Department of Justice to obtain the largest SCRA settlement in the history of the DOJ.

EPILOGUE

Hurley knocked down the door.

Sgt. James Hurley's case was the first in the history of our legal system to seat a jury for violations of the Servicemembers' Civil Relief Act. Prior to Hurley, the Justice Department's Civil Rights Division had not filed a single SCRA lawsuit to protect our military men and women when they entered active duty or were deployed. Hurley pioneered this area of the law – five years of fierce litigation – that opened the flood gates to allow the Department of Justice to recover more than $50 million for servicemembers who were harmed by illegal foreclosures or lending practices. When Assistant Attorney General Thomas Perez tried to get bipartisan support for his appointment by President Obama as Secretary of Labor, Perez referred to Hurley and the DOJ National Settlement.

Only future historians will be able to understand the dynamics between the Obama and Bush presidencies; comparing the Bush surge in Iraq and mortgage crisis, and Obama's Attorney General getting the largest SCRA settlement in the history of the DOJ.

In February 2015, the Department of Justice issued the following press release:

The Justice Department announced today that under its settlements with five of the nation's largest mortgage servicers, 952 service members and their co-borrowers are eligible to receive over $123 million for non-judicial foreclosures that violated the Servicemembers Civil Relief Act (SCRA). The five mortgage servicers are JP Morgan Chase Bank N.A. (JP Morgan Chase); Wells Fargo Bank N.A. and Wells Fargo & Co. (Wells Fargo); Citi Residential Lending Inc., Citibank, NA and CitiMortgage Inc. (Citi); GMAC Mortgage, LLC, Ally Financial Inc. and Residential Capital LLC (GMAC Mortgage); and BAC Home Loans Servicing LP formerly known as Countrywide Home Loans Servicing LP (Bank of America).

In the first round of payments under the SCRA portion of the 2012 settlement known as the National Mortgage Settlement (NMS), 666 service members and their co-borrowers will receive over $88 million from JP Morgan Chase, Wells Fargo, Citi and GMAC Mortgage. The other 286 service members and their co-borrowers are receiving over $35 million from Bank of America through an earlier settlement. The non-judicial foreclosures at issue took place between Jan. 1, 2006, and Apr. 4, 2012.

"These unlawful judicial foreclosures forced hundreds of service members and their families out of their homes," said Acting Associate Attorney General Stuart F. Delery. "While this compensation will provide a measure of relief, the fact is that service members should never have to worry about losing their home to an illegal foreclosure while they are serving our country. The department will continue to actively protect our service members and their families from such unjust actions."

"We are very pleased that the men and women of the armed forces who were subjected to unlawful non-judicial foreclosures while they were serving our country are now receiving compensation," said Acting Assistant Attorney General Vanita Gupta of the Civil Rights Division.

"We look forward, in the coming months, to facilitating the compensation of additional service members who were subjected to unlawful judicial foreclosures or excess interest charges. We appreciate that JP Morgan Chase, Wells Fargo, Citi, GMAC Mortgage and Bank of America have been working cooperatively with the Justice Department to compensate the service members whose rights were violated."

Section 533 of the SCRA prohibits non-judicial foreclosures against service members who are in military service or within the applicable post-service period, as long as they originated their mortgages before their period of military service began. Even in states that normally allow mortgage foreclosures to proceed non-judicially, the SCRA prohibits servicers from doing so against protected service members during their military service and applicable post-military service coverage period.

Under the NMS, for mortgages serviced by Wells Fargo, Citi and GMAC Mortgage, the identified service members will each receive $125,000, plus any lost equity in the property and interest on that equity. Eligible co-borrowers will also be compensated for their share of any lost equity in the property. To ensure consistency with an earlier private settlement, JP Morgan Chase will provide any identified service member either the property free and clear of any debt or the cash equivalent of the full value of the home at the time of sale, and the opportunity to submit a claim for compensation for any additional harm suffered, which will be determined by a special consultant, retired U.S. District Court Judge Edward N. Cahn.

Payment amounts have been reduced for those service members or co-borrowers who have previously received compensation directly from the servicer or through a prior settlement, such as the independent foreclosure review conducted by the Office of the Comptroller of the Currency and the Federal Reserve Board. The Bank of America payments to identified service members with nonjudicial foreclosures were made under a 2011 settlement with the Department of Justice.

The NMS also provides compensation for two categories of service members: (1) those who were foreclosed upon pursuant to a court order where the mortgage servicer failed to file a proper affidavit with the court stating whether or not the service member was in military service; and (2) those service members who gave proper notice to the servicer, but were denied the full benefit of the SCRA's 6% interest rate cap on pre-service mortgages. The service members entitled to compensation for these alleged violations will be identified later in 2015.

The following chart shows the number of service members who will be compensated by each of the servicers for the non-judicial foreclosures:

Amount of Money to be Distributed

Number of Service Members Eligible for Compensation

Bank of America	**$35,369,756**	**286**
Citi	**$14,880,578**	**126**
GMAC Mortgage	**$13,720,588**	**113**
JP Morgan Chase	**$31,068,523**	**188**
Wells Fargo	**$28,358,179**	**239**

TOTALS

$123,397,624 952

Borrowers should use the following contact information for questions about SCRA payments under the National Mortgage Settlement:

- Bank of America borrowers should call Rust Consulting, Inc., the settlement administrator, toll-free at 1-855-793-1370 or write to BAC Home Loans Servicing Settlement Administrator, c/o Rust Consulting, Inc., P.O. Box 1948, Faribault, MN 55021-6091.

- Citi borrowers should call Citi toll-free at 1-888-326-1166.

- GMAC Mortgage borrowers should call Rust Consulting Inc., the settlement administrator, toll-free at 1-866-708-0915 or write to P.O. Box 3061, Faribault, Minnesota 55021-2661.

- JPMorgan Chase borrowers should call Chase toll-free at 1-877-469-0110 or write to P.O. Box 183224, OH-7160/DOJ, Columbus, Ohio 43219-6009.

- Wells Fargo borrowers should call the Wells Fargo Home Mortgage Military Customer Service Center toll free at 1-877-839-2359.

Service members and their dependents who believe that their SCRA rights have been violated should contact an Armed Forces Legal Assistance office. To find the closest office, consult the military legal assistance office locator at **http://legalassistance.law.af.mil** and click on the Legal Services Locator. Additional information about the Justice Department's enforcement of the SCRA and the other laws protecting service members is available at **www.servicemembers.gov.**

Today's settlement was announced in connection with the President Financial Fraud Enforcement Task Force. The task force was est lished to wage an aggressive, coordinated and proactive effort vestigate and prosecute financial crimes. With more than twer eral agencies, ninety-four U.S. Attorneys' Offices and state partners, it is the broadest coalition of law enforcement, investigatory and regulatory agencies ever assembled to combat fraud. Since its formation, the task force has made great strides in facilitating increased investigation and prosecution of financial crimes, enhancing coordination and cooperation among federal, state and local authorities, addressing discrimination in the lending and financial markets and conducting outreach to the public, victims, financial institutions and other organizations.

Over the past three fiscal years, the Justice Department has filed nearly 10,000 financial fraud cases against nearly 15,000 defendants including more than 2,900 mortgage fraud defendants. For more information on the task force, please visit **www.StopFraud.gov.**

Note: The release is corrected to reflect that the other 286 service members and their co-borrowers are receiving over $35 million from Bank of America through an earlier settlement.

***

The following is Eric Halperin's (Special Counsel for Fair Lending, Civil Rights Division, Department of Justice) July, 2013 testimony:

"Good morning, Chairman Sanders, Ranking Member Burr, and Members of the Committee. Thank you for holding this hearing on preserving the rights of servicemembers, veterans and their families in the financial marketplace. It is a privilege to speak with you today about our shared priority of protecting the rights of our men and women in uniform.

Over the past four years, the Department of Justice has made enforcement of the Servicemembers Civil Relief Act (SCRA) a top priority. I am pleased to share with you today some of the recent successes we have had in working with the Department of Defense and the Office of Servicemember Affairs at the Consumer Financial Protection Bureau ensure that servicemembers' homes and credit are protected while serve our nation.

We have also learned some important lessons from our enforcement efforts over recent years and have been reviewing ways this law could be amended to better protect the rights of servicemembers.

I. SCRA ENFORCEMENT ACCOMPLISHMENTS

The Civil Rights Division enforces several laws designed to protect the rights of members of the military, including the SCRA, which provides a wide-range of protections. Among other protections, the SCRA postpones, suspends, terminates, or reduces the amount of certain consumer debt obligations for active duty members of the armed forces, so that they can focus their full attention on their military responsibilities without adverse consequences for themselves or their families. Among these protections are: (1) a prohibition on foreclosure of an active duty servicemember's property without first getting approval from the court if the servicemember obtained the loan prior to entering military service, (2) a prohibition on foreclosure of an active duty servicemember's property through a default judgment without first filing an affidavit alerting the court to the servicemember's military status, and (3) the right of a servicemember to have his or her interest rate lowered to six percent on debt that was incurred before entering military service.

These protections are in place because servicemembers should not have to worry – that their cars will be repossessed while they are on the front lines overseas, that they could lose their home, or that their spouses and children will be evicted while they are on deployment.

Enforcing these rights has been a top priority of the Division under the leadership of Attorney General Holder and former Assistant Attorney General Perez Members of the military who have made great personal sacrifices on behalf of this country should not be required to transition to civilian life only to find their credit ruined and their homes foreclosed on and sold.

In enforcing the SCRA, we have worked closely with our feder state partners. The Department of Defense has been invaluab enforcement efforts, especially our ability to bring large practice cases, and the CFPB has been an important source of information about the financial challenges facing servicemembers.

A. Wrongful Foreclosure Cases

In 2011, we reached two multi-million dollar settlements on behalf of servicemembers whose homes had been foreclosed on without court orders while they were on active duty or shortly after they had returned from active duty. The first settlement was for over

$238 million with Bank of America. The Bank of America case began with a referral from the United States Marine Corps on behalf of a servicemember who was deployed to Iraq. Bank of America was scheduled to sell that servicemember's home at a trustee's sale in three days, even though the bank had already received a copy of his military orders. In the course of our investigation and settlement negotiations, the Department found that 309 servicemembers' homes were illegally foreclosed on between 2006 and 2010. Under the consent decree, Bank of America will pay each victim a minimum of $116,785, plus compensation for any equity lost with interest.

Under our second settlement, Saxon Mortgage Services, Inc., is in the process of paying out over $2.5 million to nineteen servicemembers whose homes were unlawfully foreclosed upon between 2006 and 2010. Each servicemember will receive a minimum of $130,555, plus compensation for any equity lost with interest.

Under both settlements, the banks have agreed not to pursue any remaining amounts owed under the mortgages; to take steps to remedy negative credit reporting; and to implement enhanced measures, including monitoring, training, and checking loans against the Defense Manpower Data Center's SCRA database during the foreclosure pro-

ruary 2012, we filed consent orders with Bank of America, n Chase & Co., Wells Fargo & Company, Citigroup, Inc., and

Ally Financial, Inc. (Formerly GMAC) in United States, et al. V Bank of America Corp., et al. (D.D.C.). These consent orders are known as "the National Mortgage Settlement," which was reached by the United States, forty-nine state attorneys general, the District of Columbia and the five servicers in 2012. Under these agreements, loans serviced by the nation's five largest mortgage loan servicers are being reviewed to find all servicemembers foreclosed on either judicially or non-judicially in violation of the SCRA since 2006, and to find all servicemembers unlawfully charged interest in excess of 6% on their mortgages since 2008. As a result of these settlements, combined with the Department's other SCRA settlements, the vast majority of all foreclosures against servicemembers are now subject to court- ordered review.

Under the National Mortgage Settlement, most servicemembers wrongfully foreclosed on will receive $125,000 plus any lost equity with interest. For the foreclosure violations that took place in 2009 and 2010, the Justice Department is coordinating with the Office of the Comptroller of the Currency and the Federal Reserve Board, which are conducting separate reviews of twelve mortgage services under the Independent Foreclosure Review process.

Under the National Mortgage Settlement, Servicemembers who were denied a required reduction to a six percent interest rate will also receive a minimum of four times the amount wrongfully charged in excess of 6%. The financial compensation to servicemembers provided by the settlement is in addition to the $25 billion in relief the settlement provides to homeowners based on the servicers' illegal mortgage loan servicing practices.

Behind each of these settlements are stories of servicemembers who have made great sacrifices for our country, only to have their rights violated at home. For example, we encountered a case involving a servicemember who was severely injured by an Improvised Explosiv Device while serving in Iraq, breaking his back and causing traum brain injury. The servicer foreclosed on him, despite receiving n on multiple occasions that he was serving in Iraq. He returned United States in a wheelchair with the prognosis that he wou walk again. He spent two years in recovery, during which time he re-learned how to walk and eventually run; however, he still suffers from the impact of traumatic brain injury. Under our settlement, the servicemember received $130,651 and is eligible to have his credit report corrected to reflect that the foreclosure was not valid.

In another case, we encountered a victim who suffers from Post-Traumatic Distress Syndrome after a tour in Iraq in 2003-2004. Consequently, he regularly receives counseling and takes medication to address his nightmares and nervous condition. In an attempt to avoid foreclosure on his home, he notified the servicer of his active duty status and provided copies of his orders. However, the servicer foreclosed on him twice despite notice of protected status.

B. Wrongful Foreclosures, Repossessions and Court

Judgments; Improper Denials of Six Percent Interest Rate

In July 2012, we filed and settled United States v Capital One,

N.A. (E.D. Va), one of the most comprehensive SCRA settlements ever obtained by a government agency or any private party under the SCRA. Under the consent order, Capital One agreed to pay more than $15 million in monetary relief to resolve allegations of a variety of SCRA violations, including wrongful foreclosures, improper repossessions of motor vehicles, wrongful court judgments, improper denials of the six percent interest rate that the SCRA guarantees to servicemembers on pre-service credit card and other loans, and insufficient six percent benefits granted on credit cards, car loans and other types of accounts.

The agreement requires Capital One to pay approximately $7 million in damages to servicemembers for SCRA violations, including at least 125,000 plus compensation for any lost equity (with interest) to each vicemember whose home was unlawfully foreclosed upon, and at $10,000 plus compensation for any lost equity (with interest) h servicemember whose motor vehicle was unlawfully repos- In addition, the agreement required Capital One to create a $5 million fund to compensate servicemembers who did not receive the appropriate amount of SCRA benefits after requesting a reduction to a six percent interest rate on their credit card accounts, motor vehicle finance loans, and consumer loans.

Approximately $3 million of this fund was used as payments to servicemembers. The remaining approximately $2 million has been donated by Capital One to military emergency aid societies. Thousands of servicemembers who were victims of Capital One's unfair lending practices will be identified and compensated, with no action required on their part, for loans dating back to July 15, 2006, and those whose credit scores were damaged because Capital One violated the SCRA will have their credit scores repaired.

II. COMMENTS ON PENDING LEGISLATION

Through our enforcement work, we have achieved great successes on behalf of servicemembers, but we have also identified ways that the SCRA could be strengthened to better protect the rights of servicemembers. In September 2011, the Administration formally transmitted to Congress a package of proposals for strengthening all three statutes enforced by the Civil Rights Division that protect the rights of servicemembers and their families, including the SCRA, and we are eager to work with the Committee on these proposals. We were pleased that, last Congress, the Chairwoman Senator Patty Murray included many of our proposals in S. 2299, the "Servicemembers Rights Enforcement Improvement Act."

- These proposals, if passed, would: Double the amount of civil penalties currently available under the SCRA, to $110,000 for a first violation and $220,000 for subsequent violations;

- Codify the rule that a party seeking a default judgment against a servicemember must check Department of Defense records to determine whether the servicemember is on active duty;

- Clarify retroactive application of provisions establishing vate right of action and the authority of the Attorney Gene force the SCRA; and

- Grant civil investigative demand authority to the Attorney General to compel the production of existing documents in SCRA investigations.

When Congress amended the SCRA to provide for civil penalties in 2010, it used the amounts authorized under the Fair Housing Amendments Act. These amounts, however, have not been adjusted for inflation or for any other reason since 1999. Some violations of the SCRA involve small monetary amounts, making the civil penalty critical to ensuring compliance.

We urge the Committee to amend the SCRA's affidavit requirement, which provides that a party seeking foreclosure or other default judgment against a servicemember must first file with the court an affidavit stating whether or not the servicemember is

in military service, to clarify that such requirement includes the obligation to take reasonable steps to determine the servicemembers' military status. Such steps would include, but are not limited to, searching available Department of Defense records. The amendment would simply codify what several courts have already held.

We also urge the Committee to amend the SCRA to clarify that the private right of action and the Attorney General's authority to enforce the SCRA, which were made explicit in the Veterans' Benefits Act of 2010, apply retroactively to violations occurring before the date of enactment of that Act. This would be consistent with the Department's litigating position and with the recent decisions of the United States Court of Appeals for the Fourth Circuit, and would ensure that the SCRA rights of all servicemembers can be vindicated.

Finally, the Department urges the Committee to amend the SCRA to provide the Attorney General with civil investigative demand (CID) authority. The Department of Justice has no pre-suit investigative ity under the SCRA, and must rely on voluntary cooperation subjects of ou investigations. Greater investigative authority would strengthen the Department's ability to enforce the SCRA, especially through pattern or practice suits. In addition, the Administration has proposed as part of the FY 2014 National Defense Authorization Act to give the Department the ability to bring enforcement actions under the Military Lending Act (MLA) if violations of that Act constitute a pattern or practice or raise an issue of public importance. This is analogous to the Department's enforcement authority under the SCRA and would allow for more efficient and effective law enforcement, especially when actors are engaged in conduct that potentially violates both the MLA and the SCRA.

We will continue to work with Congress to identify areas in which additional legislative changes would improve enforcement of the SCRA and the MLA, which also extends vital economic protections to our servicemembers, and anticipate advancing additional legislative proposals this Congress.

III. LOOKING FORWARD

The Department anticipates the opportunity to report on our accomplishments in enforcing the SCRA, and to comment on our legislative proposals to strengthen the SCRA. We stand ready to work with the Committee in strengthening this important law that protects the rights of our servicemembers.

Thank you for the opportunity to testify today, and I look forward to answering your questions."

Since Hurley, there has been a $26 billion settlement between the attorney generals of forty-nine states and the District of Columbia, with Bank of America, Citibank, JPMorgan Chase, Wells Fargo and Ally Financial for U.S. Military Personnel and their families. At least $17 billion of the settlement went to modifying delinquent mortgages, with another $3 billion being used to refinance current mortgages. $5 billion went to state fines.

In April 2012, the United States Department of Defense stated more than 300 service members whose homes were unlawfully closed upon between 2006 and 2010, are due to receive more than $39 million in relief for alleged violations of the Servicemembers' Civil Relief Act.

The relief stems from the Justice Department's 2011 settlements with BAC Home Loans Servicing LP, a subsidiary of Bank of America Corp., and Saxon Mortgage Servicing Inc., a subsidiary of Morgan Stanley.

Under the first settlement, Bank of America is required to pay more than $36.8 million to service members whose homes were foreclosed upon unlawfully between 2006 and 2010. Each service member will receive a minimum of $116,785, plus compensation for any equity lost with interest. Officials said that Bank of America already has begun compensating 142 service members whose homes were illegally fore-closed on between 2006 and the middle of 2009.

Under the same agreement, Bank of America agreed to provide infor-mation about its foreclosures from mid-2009 through the end of 2010. As a result of that review, Bank of America will now pay 155 service members whose homes it illegally foreclosed on.

Borrowers who receive payment under this settlement may receive an additional payment under a settlement between Bank of America and federal banking regulators – the Office of the Comptroller of the Cur-rency and the Board of Governors of the Federal Reserve System – if the foreclosure occurred in 2009 or 2010. Payments provided under the federal banking regulators' settlement will bring the total amount received by eligible borrowers to $125,000, plus equity where appli-cable.

Under the second settlement, Saxon Mortgage Services, Inc., is in the process of paying out more than $2.5 million to nineteen service mem-bers whose homes were unlawfully foreclosed upon between 2006 and 010. Each service member will receive a minimum of $130,555.56, 's compensation for any equity lost with interest.

of America is one of five mortgage servicers that entered into a settlement, known as the National Mortgage Settlement, with the Justice Department in 2012 regarding its foreclosure practices. The Justice Department is overseeing ongoing audits of the five largest mortgage servicers in the country – Wells Fargo, Bank of America, Citibank, JP Morgan Chase and Ally – to identify violations of the Servicemembers Civil Relief Act's foreclosure provisions between Jan. 1, 2006 and April 4, 2012, and a 6 percent interest rate cap provision between Jan. 1, 2008, and April 4, 2012.

The $36.8 million being paid by Bank of America to 297 service members is pursuant to the 2011 consent decree – which predated the National Mortgage Settlement – and represents only the non-judicial foreclosures conducted by Bank of America, Justice Department officials said. As the National Mortgage Settlement audits progress, they added, the Justice Department will require payments by Bank of America for judicial foreclosure and interest rate violations, and by the other four servicers for judicial and non-judicial foreclosure and interest rate violations.

Under the National Mortgage Settlement, most service members wrongfully foreclosed on will receive $125,000 plus any lost equity. For the foreclosure violations that took place in

2009 and 2010, the Justice Department is coordinating closely with the Office of the Comptroller and the Federal Reserve Board, which are conducting separate reviews of 12 mortgage servicers under the Independent Foreclosure Review process.

"Our men and women in the military should not have to worry about a bank foreclosing on their home while they bravely serve our country,' said Eric Halperin, special counsel for fair lending in the Justice Department's civil rights division. "The Justice Department will vigorously enforce the laws that protect service members while they d their difficult and necessary work."

***

On May 7, 2013 when the Michigan Attorney General Bill Schuette and Jeff Barnes, Director of the Michigan Veteran Affairs Agency launched the Michigan Veterans Homeowners Assistance Program (MiVHAP), they stated, "the case of Sgt. James B. Hurley, a disabled veteran who lost his Hartford, Michigan home to foreclosure while serving his country in Iraq vividly illustrated the problem of lenders illegally foreclosing upon veterans. Sgt. Hurley was forced to pursue private litigation for nearly four years before settling with Deutsche Bank in 2011."

Michigan has approximately 700,000 veterans and 12,000 troops active in the Michigan National Guard. More than 22,000 Michigan National Guard members have deployed since September 11, 2001, with 300 currently deployed. The average deployment period is one year, following a two-month mobilization and training period. The Michigan Guard has some of the most actively deployed combat units in the country, with the average Michigan soldier deploying four to five times throughout their military career.

The MiVHAP will provide financial assistance to Michigan military service members, veterans and their families who have struggled with the consequences of the mortgage foreclosure crisis. Schuette and Barnes were joined at the announcement by Anne Marie Dutcher, who was administrator of the Michigan Veterans Trust Fund (the state entity charged with administering the new program).

"Our veterans and their families make sacrifices to protect the freedoms we hold dear, and they should never be forced out of their homes illegally," said Schuette. "Veterans have special protections from foreclosure under the law, but in many cases those protections were ignored by lenders, who pursued improper foreclosures. This new assistance is an important step toward restoring the lives of Great Lakes State Veterans who may have struggled to keep their homes during the foreclosure crisis."

is an important collaboration with the Attorney General, the challenges of deployment including the tempo of operation and the difficulty with establishing communications during normal business hours with lenders, makes it almost impossible for

soldiers to remedy a pending foreclosure from the field," said Barnes. "Further, the ramifications of foreclosure may also result in the soldier losing their security clearance, creating a problem with their military job and can render them ineligible for redeployment. Foreclosure for military service members continues to create additional problems for years by creating barriers to civilian employment and future home ownership."

Federal regulators and court settlements have documented approximately 900 service members nationwide who were foreclosed upon in violation of the federal Servicemembers' Civil Relief Act. At least 6,000 more were overcharged during the crisis by JP Morgan.

Supported Viewpoint from Attorney and Author James Ford

James Ford is a highly respected attorney in Kalamazoo, Michigan and second-generation Air Force pilot. His father, John was an Air Force pilot during World War II, and Ford flew sixty-five combat missions as an Air Force pilot in Vietnam. His legal career has been just as honorable. He chronicled the life of his wonderful family in the book, *I Lived in Those Times: Five Generations of a Michigan Pioneer Family* (2009, Fortitude Publishing). In the book, he shares of his life as an attorney and describes litigation as a "knife fight." The behavior of the defense attorneys in the Hurley case can be better understood when reading about the insurance defense attorneys James described in his book:

"[a] lawyer who works full time for an insurance company is under enormous pressure to do whatever it takes to win his case. If he resists on ethical grounds there are plenty of others with fewer scruples who will be happy to take his place. What the insurance company wants is victory. How the lawyer gets it is his problem....Insurance companie use shady tactics because there is virtually no penalty when they caught. Usually the worst that happens is that they have to pay they owe, and if the tactics work they pay nothing." Not only we defense attorneys running up their meter, they had to keep the flood-gates closed for their clients.

"We call ourselves a country of laws, and not men, but it is a false boast. So long as men interpret the laws their biases will mean more than the Constitution or any law passed by the legislature" (page 537). This statement equally applies to what happened to Hurley's odyssey through the judicial system.

Conservative Republicans, captains of business and industry blame all of this on the trial lawyers. They will argue "frivolous lawsuit", or "trial lawyers are just lining their pockets."

Ford describes such nonsense in his book:

"I didn't win every case, but over the years either settled or won most of the cases I filed, because I tried to be extremely careful to only take cases that were legitimate. All competent trial lawyers follow that rule. Taking a case that is frivolous is a short road to the poor house. Insurance companies like to make noise about frivolous cases, but any lawyer who takes one is a fool. He won't win, and he will lose a lot of time and money in the process. There are fools in this profession, but they don't stay around long."

There needs to be some middle ground one would believe. Obviously, there is a need to give the third branch of the U.S. Government some serious attention. Most crucial, is the dire emergency for judicial reform in Michigan as proclaimed by former Chief Justice of the Michigan Supreme Court, Elizabeth A. Weaver in her book, *Judicial Deceit: Tyranny and Unnecessary Secrecy at the Michigan Supreme Court*, which was coauthored with David B. Schock.

Justice Weaver describes the corruption through her fellow justices' behavior.

I witnessed what's happened. And so I'm telling what I experienced. iew it as a very serious issue: our culture is in danger – our country, civilization. Part of that danger – in too many places – is the lack of an open, independent, and unbiased judiciary. I follow as true Mary Baker Eddy's Bible-based admonition '...designate those as unfaithful stewards who have seen the danger and yet have given no warning.'"

Ford describes the consequences of what Justice Weaver discloses:

"There are a thousand ways for judges to put their thumbs on the scales of justice when they want to. If a judge is afraid that a jury might decide a fact the wrong way he can simply declare that a question of fact is a question of law, and then make the decision himself. The Constitution says that juries must decide questions of fact, but if a judge just calls it a question of law he doesn't have to worry about pesky juries. The Michigan Supreme Court is a master at that game, a very few cases get to a jury under their rule.

It wasn't always that way. Up until 1999, the Michigan Supreme Court was more or less neutral. It tended to be somewhat conservative, with corporations and insurance companies winning over 50% of the cases, but only slightly, something like 53%-47%. That changed overnight in January 1999, when two Democratic Justices retired, and the Republicans gained a five to two advantage.

In the year that followed, corporations and insurance companies won 93% of their cases in front of the Michigan Supreme Court, and the numbers haven't changed much since. Over the last nine years, the Court has been so highly partisan in protecting their business interests that private individuals have had virtually no chance.

The outrageous decisions by this Court are too numerous to list, but a few examples can give some indication of how they operate. In premises liability cases the Court has forbidden any claim where the danger is "open and obvious", although no such language appears in the statute. On the surface that sounds like a reasonable rule, until one sees how it has been enforced.

According to the Court, anything visible to the naked eye is deemed open and obvious as a matter of law. In other words, the Court w· decide not a jury. Clear water on a title floor is open and obvious cause it is not impossible to see. A hole in a walkway at night is open and obvious because it would have been visible during the day, so why should there be a different rule for the nighttime hours. Water on the floor should be open and obvious to a blind man, because it isn't the restaurant owner's fault that the blind man can't see.

These are all actual cases.

A few years ago the Michigan Legislature passed a law giving a woman the right to sue if a physician negligently injures her by failing to diagnose breast cancer, thereby depriving her of a chance to survive. Then the Michigan Supreme Court got its hand on it. A woman dying of breast cancer can't sue, said the Court, because cancer isn't an "injury." Only death is an injury. She therefore must wait until after she is dead to sue. Of course if she doesn't die within two years of the date of misdiagnosis then the case is barred by the statute of limitations.

There is also a state statute requiring road commissions to maintain highways in a condition reasonably safe for travel. But if they design a defectively dangerous highway they get a free pass according to the Court. After all, the statute says, the road commission must "maintain" a safe highway. It doesn't say they have to design or build a safe highway. Even if the road commission knows the highway is defectively designed, it still has no duty to fix it because that can't be considered maintenance.

There is also no duty for the road commission to maintain traffic lights or stop signs. According to this Court traffic signs and signals aren't part of the "highway," so as a matter of law road commissions have no duty to repair them. In Michigan you'd better be careful when you approach an intersection.

The Michigan Civil Rights Act makes it illegal for employers to sexually harass female employees, but when a female employee was harassed and eventually killed because her coworkers did not like women the Court gave the employer a free pass, concluding that the statute only prohibits sexual advances. There is nothing in that statute, ruled the Court, that prevents an employer from harassing women so long as he does it out of hate instead of lust.

This is just the tip of the iceberg. The Michigan Supreme Court claims that it is just interpreting statutes literally, but it is like Humpty Dumpty in Alice in Wonderland; words mean what the Court says they mean. There is an old story about Abraham Lincoln regaling his colleagues when he was riding the circuit in Illinois. According to legend he asked his friends how many legs a horse would have if you called its tail a leg. "Five," they responded.

"Not so," said Lincoln. "No matter what you call a tail it is still a tail." But in Michigan words almost always mean that corporations win, and individuals lose. There aren't any Lincolns on the Michigan Supreme Court.

It's a court that also takes umbrage at criticism, as I discovered shortly after the Republican members took control in 1999. After a fifteen year battle the court rules in one of my cases that an automobile insurer in Michigan was not required to cover its insured driver when he was driving someone else's vehicle. The Court made that ruling despite the clear language of the statute that requires insurance companies to cover their policyholders whenever they drive "a motor vehicle." "A" motor vehicle, the court concluded, could only mean the insured's own vehicle. So once again words meant what the Court said they meant, and not what the dictionary or the legislature said they meant.

A dissenting Republican justice called the decision unconscionable, and when I was contacted by a newspaper, I went even further, calling the decision absurd. I also said that, "Until widows and orphans can donate as much money as insurance companies we will continue to see these types of decisions."

My comments were not appreciated by the Republican majority on the Court, or by their Republican friends. The Republican members of the Court and their corporate sponsors had worked a long time to gai control of Michigan's legal system, and they didn't want criticism jeopardize what they had attained. So a couple weeks after my comments appeared in the paper my secretary, Amy Arver, was waiting for me when I returned from lunch. "The Supreme Court didn't like what you said," she told me, as she handed me a grievance from the Michigan Attorney Grievance Commission."

Post Hurley SCRA Michigan Cases

The cases of a combat sergeant, an Army captain, and a retired Army drill sergeant are most relevant to the Hurley case, who too had lost their homes while serving in the military. The combat sergeant was the recipient of a Purple Heart, a veteran of three wars, and had completed multiple tours in each war as a combat soldier. During his case, when oral arguments on Defendants' Motion to dismiss the case were presented, his attorney began a very brief overview of the soldier's service and his case.

The presiding Federal judge in Detroit (on the record) interrupted to ask the attorney if he, "wanted the flag" that sat behind the judge in the courtroom? This soldier's attorney indicated that it was, "one of the most insulting things I have heard anyone say in a courtroom; particularly given the context...I will happily go down on record as calling that judge a very bad person for that comment forever." Ironically, that same judge currently sits on a panel to instruct attorneys on how to be civil and professional in the courtroom, and in their dealings with other attorneys and judges.

Following oral arguments, this judge dismissed the sergeant's case. The sergeant appealed to the 6th Circuit Court of Appeals in Cincinnati, Ohio. However, while the sergeant went off to fight for his country and the protections it affords, the Court chose to hear the appeal without the benefit of oral argument. In an unusual move, the Court started to hear appeals without allowing oral arguments. The sergeant, a veteran of three wars, was not given his day in court.

another case, an Army captain was called to service after the 9/11 attacks. After serving his country, and believing that his time in the military was over, he was again called back into service years later. He was on active duty for more than five years. During that time, Citimortgage violated his rights under the SCRA on numerous occasions. Despite the fact Citimortgage was held accountable through class action settlements (all of which were similar to the types of violations they committed and continue to commit against him), the judges in Bay City refused to follow the Act. The Court's actions and rulings in Bay City concerning the captain's rights under the SCRA could be an entire book, in and of itself.

The final example is one of a former Army drill sergeant who had proudly served his country for more than twenty-nine years. While on active duty, the bank foreclosed on his home, evicted him from the residence, and threw all of his personal belongings onto a curb in Detroit. Not only did the sergeant return from his active duty service efforts and find himself homeless, he was arrested after someone had taken and illegally used information about his identity from the personal papers that were tossed on the curb.

On a case of first impression, and before discovery could even be conducted, a Federal Judge in Ann Arbor, Michigan, dismissed the complaint. The judge found that the sergeant's claims were barred by the applicable Statute of Limitations; a statute of limitations that was not applicable to mortgage foreclosures, real property, or consumer protections. Rather, this judge found that the sergeant's claims were similar to Michigan conversion (even though conversion pertains to personal property only).

The judge's decision provided more time for consumers to bring a cause of action against a company for a defective home appliance, than the time allowed for a soldier to bring a cause of action against a financial institution who had left him homeless. The judge's actions were a violation of the SCRA.

At the state level, Attorney Matt Cooper was told by a District Court judge to "get off [his] soapbox", as he tried to stop a financial institution from evicting the family of a deployed servicemember. All of this causes one to reflect about what Colonel Odom said when Matt drove him to the airport for his departure from Michigan for the last time, "I hope to never again come back to the State of Michigan." What is it about the culture and the state of judiciary at both the federal and state level that has caused this to happen in the once great State of Michigan?

***

As a result of Hurley being such a significant landmark case, Matt is regularly requested to help servicemembers and their families. Recognizing the need for assistance for the men and women serving our county, Matt Cooper, Lisa Hudson and Frank Melchiore have founded the Servicemembers Civil Relief Act Foundation, Inc. **www.SCRAFoundation.org.**

ABOUT THE AUTHOR

Attorney Matthew R. Cooper made national headlines as the lead litigator in the landmark case known as the Hurley Case. Cooper represented Sgt. James Hurley, an Iraq War Veteran from Hartford, Michigan in a courtroom battle against Wall Street that would forever protect the rights of all personnel serving in the United States Military. His actions effectuated amendments by Congress to the Servicemembers' Civil Relief Act.

The Hurley case appeared on the front page of *The New York Times*, and other major newspapers around the world. It eventually caught the attention of the *CBS Evening News,* where Katie Couric interviewed Cooper, alongside Gen. David Patraeus and his wife, Holly Patraeus.

For more than twenty-five years, he has represented clients in major litigation cases, and has participated in jury trials in Michigan's Van Buren, Kalamazoo, Barry, and Wayne counties. He has prosecuted cases in Illinois, Maryland, Indiana, and Michigan at the Federal and State Court levels, and has appeared in Circuit Court in over seventeen Michigan Counties. Cooper has handled cases in the Western and Eastern Federal District Courts, the United States 6th Circuit Court of Appeals, the Michigan Court of Appeals, and the Michigan Supreme Court.

He graduated cum laude from Western Michigan University with a bachelor's degree in public administration, political science. Cooper's career took off after he graduated with honors in Contracts and Criminal Law from Valparaiso University School of Law in Valparaiso, Indiana. He began work as clerk for a Circuit Court judge, and moved on to join the Law Offices of Schuitmaker, Cooper, Cypher & Knotek, P.C.

He and his wife Laurie, reside on a small farm in Paw Paw, Michigan with their children Anella, Drew and Bennett, and their loyal companion Buck.

Cooper, along with attorney Frank B. Melchiore, and Lisa A. Hudson, founded the Servicemembers Civil Relief Act (SCRA) Foundation. The foundation has pioneered the modern-day application of this area of the law. Together, they laid the groundwork for the United States Department of Justice to obtain the largest SCRA settlement in its history.

The day the United States District Court found that the federally protected rights of U. S. Army Sgt. James Hurley were violated was a mammoth victory for our Nation's Servicemembers and their families' efforts to protect their homes.

That day happened because of the unwavering vision, selfless toil, and perseverance in the face of often vicious adversity confronted by Matt Cooper; a small-town lawyer with the heart of a thousand lions. He would not quit. He did not quit. As with our Servicemembers and their families, Matt truly deserves our unending respect.

Frank Melchiore, J. D., Pirate, St. Petersburg, Florida

For more information, visit: www.scrafoundation.org.

Made in the USA
San Bernardino, CA
11 September 2016